THE MANY FACES
OF JUDAISM

THE MANY FACES OF JUDAISM

Orthodox, Conservative, Reconstructionist & Reform

GILBERT S. ROSENTHAL

Edited by Seymour Rossel

**BEHRMAN HOUSE, INC.
NEW YORK**

© Copyright 1978 by Gilbert S. Rosenthal
Published by Behrman House, Inc., 1261 Broadway, New York, N.Y. 10001
Manufactured in the United States of America

Library of Congress Cataloging in Publication Data

Rosenthal, Gilbert S
    The many faces of Judaism.

    Bibliography: p. 160.
    1. Judaism—United States.   2. Orthodox
Judaism—United States.   3. Reform Judaism—United
States.   4. Conservative Judaism.   5. Reconstructionist
Judaism. I. Title.
BM205. R595   296′.0973   78-25898
ISBN 0-87441-311-7

Designed by Ed Schneider/Photo Editing by Tricia Grantz

Photographs courtesy of: Congregation Beth El-Zedeck, Indianapolis, p. 127. Temple Emanu-El,
N.Y.C., p. 66, 78, 80, 87, 88, 115. Culver Pictures, p. 14. International Museum of Photography,
Rochester, N.Y. At George Eastman House, p. 21. Hebrew Union College-Jewish Institute of Religion,
American Jewish Archives, p. 72, 93. Hebrew Union College-Jewish Institute of Religion, p. 61, 63, 70,
73, 75, 115. Library of Congress, p. 11. Jewish Theological Seminary, p. 52, 68, 95, 99, 100, 101, 103,
104, 108, 110. N.Y. State Library, p. 13. Reconstructionist Foundation, p. 119, 124, 125, 126, 127, 131,
134. Religious News Service, p. 6, 43, 71, 75, 99, 102, 143. Seymour Rossel, p. 76. Stephen Wise Free
Synagogue, N.Y.C.-Alayne Zatulove, p. 71, 74. Stephen Wise Free Synagogue, p. 76. Union of
American Hebrew Congregations, p. 72. United Synagogue Review, p. 102. Yeshiva University Photo
Library, p. 19, 28, 31, 39, 40, 41, 43, 50; Private Collection N.Y. p. 37; On permanent loan to Yeshiva
University Museum by the National Council of Young Israel, N.Y.C. p. 47.

For the Teller family of Israel,
builders of Jerusalem
and the Jewish State.

CONTENTS

THE MANY FACES
OF JUDAISM

AMERICAN JUDAISM

The American Jewish Community may be the largest and most powerful Jewish community in history. More Jews live in America today than in the Land of Israel in the days of the Second Temple, or in the land of Babylonia in the days when the Talmud was written, or in Germany before the Second World War, or in Poland in the days of the Shtetl. There are nearly six million of us, the largest concentration of Jews ever gathered together in one country at one time. And we are spread over a huge geographic area ranging from Alaska to Florida, from Maine to Hawaii.

The Jews of America are also the wealthiest and most influential Jewish community in modern times. Of course not all American Jews are wealthy; in fact, there are many poor Jews—some estimates run as high as one half million. But the average income of Jews in the United States is probably higher than that of any other religious group. Many Jews are successful businesspeople, lawyers, physicians, dentists, accountants, scientists, and professors. We are generous when it come to *tzedakah* (charity): The United Jewish Appeal and Federations of Jewish Philanthropies receive over $600 million every year, and Jews support many other charities and institutions in addition.

Politically, America's Jews have been very active. We have seen Jewish senators and representatives in Congress, Supreme Court justices, members of Presidents' cabinets, state governors, and ambassadors. It was rare for a Jew to hold a high government office in Germany or France before World War II, and almost impossible in Poland or Czarist Russia or the Moslem countries. It is unheard of in Soviet Russia today.

Even the institutions that American Jews have built are impressive. There are approximately four thousand synagogues in the United States, four major rabbinical seminaries and several minor ones, almost four hundred all-day religious schools and yeshivot and several thousand Sunday and Hebrew schools. American Jewry has established hundreds of Jewish centers and YMHAs as well as many summer camps. And all this has been created in little more than three centuries of Jewish life.

The Russian Jewish immigrant of the 1890s came to America carrying all his possessions and dreaming of a new life.

The development of Jewish life and society in America did not come about overnight, however. The process was slow—painfully slow at first—and it is only in the last century that American Jewry has come of age.

BEGINNINGS

The earliest migration of Jews came from the West Indies. Most were *Sephardim*—Spanish and Portuguese Jews—who had fled the cruel Inquisition in their native lands and were searching for religious freedom. The Catholic Church discouraged Jewish religious life in many parts of Europe throughout the persecution of the Inquisition. And when the Spanish and Portuguese monarchs expelled or forcibly converted their Jewish subjects in 1492 and 1497, respectively, Jewish life became dangerous and nearly impossible in those lands. Jews first fled to free places such as Holland, Turkey, and Italy. But not long after, when the New World was opened to colonists, they made their way to the West Indies and to Dutch and British colonies such as Recife, Curaçao, Surinam, and Barbados. By the seventeenth century there were flourishing Jewish communities in these places.

When these colonies were conquered by the intolerant Portuguese and Spanish, the Jews were forced to flee for their lives once again. True, they could have remained and become "New Christians," but most wished to live as free people and as practicing Jews. And that is how they came to the American colonies. In 1654 a boatload of twenty-three refugees from Recife, Brazil, arrived in New Amsterdam and laid the foundation for the first great American Jewish community.

Most of the immigrants were poor Sephardim. They had lost practically everything in the West Indies. Among them, too, was a sprinkling of Ashkenazic Jews originally from Germany and Holland. But all were united by one common hope: to build a new life as free men and women, as Jews.

12

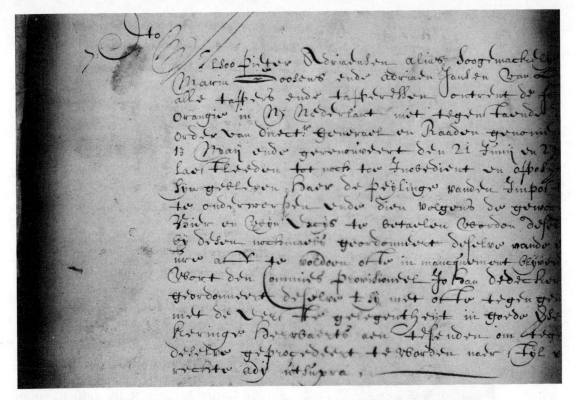

When Stuyvesant refused to allow the Jews to stand watch, two Jews—Jacob Barsimson and Asser Levy—took the case to the local government. The Journal entry for November 5, 1665, records in Dutch the decision of the government: No. But Levy and Barsimson were not dismayed. They sent their request to the Dutch West Indies Company in Holland which sent back an order to Stuyvesant: Yes. A few years later, Asser Levy was the first Jew to become a full citizen of New Amsterdam.

THE JEWS IN NEW AMSTERDAM

There were obstacles. Governor Peter Stuyvesant was not happy about letting in these poor non-believers. He accused them of dishonest business practices and deceit; denounced them as heretics, people who denied the divinity of Jesus. But the Dutch West India Company, which had established the New Amsterdam community, ordered Stuyvesant to accept the newcomers on the condition that they not become a burden to the community because of poverty, that they live in a separate area away from the Christians, and that they not conduct public prayer services. The Jews were also barred from certain businesses and trade, from standing watch at the fort, and serving in the militia. Instead of this military service, the Jews were required to pay a tax. It was not a very hopeful beginning!

The East European immigrant saw any job as an opportunity for "getting ahead"—even selling apples on the streetcorner.

But Jews fought hard for fair treatment and equal rights. After all, they had initially enjoyed freedom and equality in the Dutch West Indies. Why not in New Amsterdam as well? So they insisted upon and won the right to stand guard duty. And after the British took over the colony and renamed it New York, Jews continued to fight for more rights.

At first the British would not allow any synagogues, but in 1695 a synagogue was built in New York. In 1740 the British passed a law that enabled all foreign-born colonists to become citizens after living in New York for seven years. Moreover, this law, the Naturalization Act of 1740, stated that a citizen was no longer required to take a Christian oath. So the Jews living in New York were all able to become citizens of the British Empire.

Curiously, when the British Parliament passed a similar law in 1753 to naturalize foreigners in England, a storm of anti-Semitic protest broke loose, and the law had to be repealed the following year. As a result, the Jews in the motherland were considered foreigners for another century and not allowed to vote or hold office, while the Jews in the colonies were accepted as citizens by 1740.

The American Revolution carried the process of freedom still further. After the Constitution was ratified in 1789, the federal government made it clear that there would be no established church for the new nation, that all religious groups would be treated equally, and that church and state would be forever separate. The Bill of Rights guaranteed that the government could not abridge or limit the free exercise of any religious faith. These new guarantees of freedom gave the nearly three thousand Jews living in the United States a real reason to rejoice.

In the first half of the nineteenth century large numbers of Jews from Germany, Austria, and Bohemia arrived in America. Many were fleeing the Napoleonic wars; many were disillusioned after the failures of the revolutions of 1830 and 1848 in France, Germany, Italy, Hungary, and other European nations as liberals tried to overthrow the monarchies; many wanted to breathe free; and some just wanted to earn a better living.

There was even a sprinkling of Galician and Polish Jews among these settlers (Haym Solomon, who had helped the Revolutionary cause, came from Poland). By the time of the Civil War in 1861, American Jews numbered more than 150,000. The vast majority were Ashkenazim.

The Jews of eastern Europe followed. After the brutal May Laws of the Russian Czar Alexander III and the ruthless pogroms, or attacks, on Jews that occurred in 1881, a huge wave of Russian Jews fled to these shores. They were joined by Rumanian Jews fleeing an evil tyranny in their land. Polish, Hungarian, and Galician Jews joined the immigration of their Russian and Rumanian coreligionists. Between 1881 and 1924 two and a half million Jews, mainly from eastern Europe, came to the "Golden Land." In 1924 the U.S. Congress enacted strict immigration quotas and the great wave of Jewish immigration ceased. But the nature and composition of the American Jewish community had changed forever.

One final, smaller wave of immigration came in the wake of Nazi terror and World War II. About 150,000 Jews were able to flee before the trap closed in 1940. Another 100,000 came after the war. They were survivors of the Holocaust, mostly from eastern Europe, and included a large number of ultra-Orthodox and Hasidic Jews. Immigration and natural population growth slowly brought the number of Jews in America to the present six million. Ironically, six million Jews were destroyed in Europe, and six million worked to create a new life in America.

15

THE STRUGGLE FOR ACCEPTANCE

Jews were not readily accepted into American society. There were problems and pitfalls, legal obstacles and social barriers to overcome. America was not Europe, but it was not an ideal democracy either.

The poison of European bigotry and anti-Semitism was carried to this land by immigrants who could not shed their racist attitudes. We have already seen how Peter Stuyvesant tried his best to exclude the Jews from New Amsterdam. Unfortunately, he was not alone, and anti-Semitism was present in many communities. Most of the original thirteen colonies had established official churches (usually the Anglican Church), and they were intolerant of nonmembers, whom they denounced as being nonbelievers or heretics. The Pilgrims of New England were particularly intolerant of other religious groups and drove them from Massachusetts. In Maryland a Jew named Dr. Lumbrozo was actually tried and came close to being burned at the stake in 1658 for denying the Godhood of Jesus. Even after the Constitution was adopted, the individual states were still empowered to set their own rules regarding who could vote and who could hold office. And while Jews in New York and Pennsylvania voted and held office even before the Revolution, Jews in Maryland, North Carolina, and New Hampshire were not so fortunate. These states insisted that a public official had to swear a Christian oath before being allowed to take office. It was not until 1878 that the last of these discriminatory oaths was abolished.

But religious tolerance has always been an American ideal. The federal government never allowed prejudice on the basis of religion: The United States Constitution addresses itself equally to Christians and Jews. When six synagogues congratulated George Washington on his election to office in 1789, the President wrote: "Happily, the Government of the United States, which gives to bigotry no sanction, to persecution no assistance, requires only that they who live under its protection should demean themselves as good citizens. . . ." Thomas Jefferson wrote to the American Jewish leader Major Mordecai M. Noah, saying that our laws have applied the only antidote to religious intolerance by "protecting our religious rights, as they do our civil rights, by putting all on an equal footing." Unlike nations such as Germany, Italy, Russia, Poland, and Spain, America never had an official anti-Semitic policy and never has passed an anti-Semitic or anti-Jewish law.

America began as a pluralistic country with many diverse groups, sects, nationalities, and ethnic blocs. In fact, there are more than 250 religious sects in the United States today. Consequently, the addition of one more group—the Jews—was not disturbing to the rest. Because Americans are

16

not dogmatic or fanatic about religion, Jews have been accepted. A Jew does not have to convert to rise to the top. In America it is possible to become a Supreme Court justice or secretary of state and yet remain a Jew.

Because of this mood of religious liberalism and moderation, voluntarism and pluralism, American Jews have made great strides without the aid of official laws or pronouncements. Apart from the Naturalization Act of 1740 which gave Jews the opportunity to become full-fledged citizens, it was the social climate of American life which generally brought about change. In Europe, official laws and acts of parliament were required to emancipate the Jews; in America, almost from the start the Jews were a part of the mainstream of political, economic, and social life.

Naturally, there have been struggles, even in our own time. Jews are sometimes excluded from certain occupations, housing areas, and social and athletic clubs. Until fairly recently, there were quota systems in colleges and graduate schools, and there were few Jewish professors on campuses. For a long time it was terribly difficult for Jewish students to get into medical schools. But in the last twenty-five years the situation has improved greatly, even though anti-Semitism has not been totally eliminated from American life.

PROBLEMS OF CHURCH AND STATE

The problem of church and state has been thorny and persistent. Many early Christian settlers considered America a "Christian" nation. Consequently, Protestants sought to make their communities Christian settlements. Prayers were introduced into the public schools, the "Blue Laws" forced businesses to close on Sunday, and several state constitutions actually referred to the state as a "Christian" settlement. Many rabbis and Jewish leaders fought this trend.

A decision of the Supreme Court in 1963 called prayers in the public schools unconstitutional. But Christmas observances are still popular in schools, and Nativity scenes showing the birth of Jesus are often found in public places. The Sunday Blue Laws have virtually disappeared because of businesspeople's desire for more work days, but bitterness still lingers among some Christian groups who urge that prayer be restored to the schools and

Sunday be the official Sabbath.

Another church-state problem not yet settled is whether state or federal aid should be given to parochial or private schools. For many years Jewish groups resisted any public funding of private and parochial schools partly because they wanted to keep religion and state separate and partly because they believed that once the government gives money to a school or institution it will interfere with the policies of that institution. But as the number of students in Jewish day schools has risen to almost eighty thousand, and as the costs of education have soared, the Orthodox Jewish community joined by some Conservative and Reform rabbis has called for the government to aid even the private schools.

SHAPING RELIGIOUS INSTITUTIONS

From our earliest days religious institutions were vitally important to Jews. Wherever they settled they set up synagogues and schools, cemeteries and *mikvaot* (ritual baths), as well as charities and societies to help Jews observe the *mitzvot* (commandments). It has been the same in America. No sooner did the Jews arrive than they struggled to create the institutions of Jewish life. It did not matter that the community of New Amsterdam refused to allow Jews to worship publicly. Worship services were conducted in private homes instead. They purchased land for a cemetery, set up a *mikvah*, opened a *talmud torah* (a religious school) to train their children, baked *matzah* for Passover, arranged to have *kosher*-slaughtered meat and fowl, and established various charities to help Jews at home and abroad.

Nor was New York's Jewish experience unique. The same happened in Charleston, Newport, Savannah, Richmond, Philadelphia, and—a little later—in Montreal.

Interestingly, the early synagogues chanted the service according to Sephardic custom, even though by 1729 the majority of synagogue members were Ashkenazim. Perhaps this was because the Sephardim were here first and the newer settlers were reluctant to change the established customs. Or maybe the richer, more established Sephardim were able to maintain their practices

Rising above the crowded streets of New York's Lower East Side, the synagogues were the most impressive buildings. This one was built in 1896.

because of their wealth and power. In any case, it was not until 1802 that the Philadelphia Ashkenazim opened their first synagogue, Rodeph Shalom, and broke away from the Sephardic congregation, Mikveh Israel. The same happened in New York in 1825 with the funding of B'nai Jeshurun. These synagogues marked the end of Sephardic control and the rapid growth of German, Dutch, Hungarian, Polish, and other east European synagogues in America.

Of course America was a voluntaristic society where a person had the right but not the obligation to join a religious group. However, membership in the congregation was necessary if a Jew wanted to marry in the synagogue or be buried in its cemetery. Even so, synagogue membership was not as important in America as it had been in Europe.

For one thing, there were many different synagogues among which to choose. Religious activities such as cemetery control, the baking of matzah and the koshering of meat passed into private hands, too, and the strength of the synagogues further declined. By the time of the Civil War the synagogue-centered community was fragmented and weakened. Secular organizations such as B'nai B'rith appeared, religious functions such as *shehitah* (kosher slaughtering) were no longer controlled by the synagogue, and Jews pulled away from religious affiliation and observance.

America's Jews followed the Protestant pattern rather than the Catholic system. This meant that there was no chief rabbi, no *kehillah* or formal community, and no power to enforce religious decisions once the old Sephardic monopoly was shattered. Each congregation was independent and could do as it saw fit. But many Jews interpreted this freedom as license to break away from the congregation entirely.

The community was further weakened because there were no professional clergy or teachers in America before 1840. Imagine: For almost two hundred years of its existence, American Jewry had no ordained rabbi to lead them! The men who conducted services were *hazzanim* (cantors) and self-educated lay teachers. They were well meaning, but not often well schooled. Even the *shohetim* (ritual slaughterers) and *mohalim* (ritual circumcisors) were often untrained for their jobs. Difficult questions about the rituals had to be addressed to rabbis in London or Amsterdam. Except for occasional visitors, such as Rabbi Haim Caragal of Palestine who spent some time in Newport, there were really no learned Jews or scholars in America until Rabbi Abraham Rice arrived in Baltimore in 1840.

Why didn't ordained rabbis settle here sooner? For one thing, religious European Jews considered America to be a wilderness and did not wish to come here. For another, they were fearful of the dangers of a long ocean

20

Work for the new immigrants from East Europe might mean going daily to a sweatshop or staying home to toil from dawn to dark. This family sewed together men's garters to make ends meet.

voyage and the still uncivilized New World. Nor were they anxious to live so far from the great European academies of Jewish learning in an era when communications and transportation were so slow. Many rabbis viewed America as *galut,* or exile; many considered it a dumping ground for debtors and criminals; and, as recently as the beginning of the twentieth century, more than one east European sage described America as a *trefa medinah* —an unholy land.

This scarcity of rabbis caused American Jewry to suffer spiritually. The level of ritual observance and knowledge was low. By the time of the Revolution at least 10 percent of the Jewish population had married non-Jews, and by the start of the Civil War there were practically no Jewish descendants of the original pioneers. Over and over the officers of New York's Shearith Israel congregation and Philadelphia's Mikveh Israel warned Jews who ate nonkosher food or opened their shops on the Sabbath that they would lose their synagogue privileges. But these warnings did not help. Foreign visitors were amazed to see American Jews eating pork and working on the Sabbath. Jewish pack peddlars found that they had to forget about *shabbat* rules if they wanted to survive in the wilderness. In 1783 Haym Solomon wrote in a letter to his family in Poland that "Jewish life is very weak." Rabbi Rice of Baltimore was

The Jews of New York in 1877—mostly Germans who had come in the 1840s—had good reason to celebrate by holding this Purim Ball for charity. In a few short years they had grown prosperous and even wealthy in their new land.

so upset by the low level of religious observance that he wondered whether Jewish life could ever survive in America. And Reform rabbis such as Issac Mayer Wise and Max Lilienthal tried in vain to convince merchants to close their shops on Saturday.

Little by little things improved as German and Bohemian rabbis came to settle in the New World. Reverend Isaac Leeser of Philadelphia set up the first rabbinical school in America, Maimonides College, in 1867. Although it lasted but a few years, it did ordain three men. Then Isaac Mayer Wise founded the Hebrew Union College in Cincinnati in 1875. It survived and is still training rabbis and teachers today. After the huge influx of east European Jews in the 1880s, Jewish institutions proliferated. In 1886 the Jewish Theological Seminary was created in New York and the Rabbi Isaac Elchanan Theological Seminary was founded in 1897 (this became Yeshiva University). Rabbis and teachers emigrated here as synagogues and schools dotted the land.

In 1875 there were 270 synagogues, nearly all of which were Reform. By 1916 the number of synagogues had grown to an amazing 1,900—mostly Polish or Russian. A variety of Hebrew and Yiddish books, newspapers, and journals were being published. American Jewry seemed to be coming of age.

mericans normally consider themselves a religious, God-fearing people. In fact, about 90 percent of them believe in God. Of course they do not always act as if they believed in God—only about 40 percent go to church weekly—but they definitely consider themselves believers.

Much the same is true of American Jews. Few consider themselves secularists or nonbelievers. In fact, only 4.1 percent describe themselves as atheists (deniers of God) or agnostics (those who question the existence of God). The large majority of American Jews—about 82 percent—define themselves in religious terms: 40.5 percent are Conservative, 30 percent are Reform, 11.4 percent are Orthodox, and a small number are Reconstructionist. But only 50 percent of all the Jews in America are members of a synagogue, and a mere 16 percent of American Jews attend synagogue weekly.

Clearly, the American Jewish community is split into several major movements, just as its Christian neighbors are split among many different churches. This division has caused disharmony and disunity among the Jews, but it has also enriched Jewish life and thought and made American Jewry an exciting and lively community. What are the different movements? How did they develop? Who are the men and women who shaped the various schools of thought? What does each movement stand for? What are its basic teachings and practices?

This is the study that we now begin.

ORTHODOX JUDAISM

TRADITIONAL JUDAISM IN A NEW SETTING

The oldest form of Judaism in America is Orthodox Judaism. In fact, Orthodoxy was the only type of religious Judaism in this country until the 1800s, when the Reform movement began to grow. The word "Orthodox" means "right belief," and it was applied to Jews who firmly refused to change their beliefs and observances when they came to the New World. However, it may not be quite the right word to describe the Orthodox. Some people have pointed out that the Orthodox are less concerned with "right belief" than they are with observing the *mitzvot*, so the movement should really be called "Orthopraxy" or "right practice." Others in the Orthodox group argue that their way is the truly "traditional" way, and they like to call themselves "Traditional" Jews. There are even some Orthodox Jews who believe that Orthodoxy is the *only* true Judaism, and would prefer to call themselves simply "Jews." But for the most part, the term "Orthodox" has stuck.

Orthodoxy was brought to America by the earliest settlers. It was the only form of Judaism they knew. Since most of them were Sephardic Jews, they used the old Sephardic rituals in conducting their worship services, in observing holidays, and in pronouncing Hebrew. For almost 150 years this Sephardic style was accepted even by the Ashkenazim and was the "American" pattern. As more German, English, Dutch, Bohemian, and Polish Jews came to America toward the end of the eighteenth and the beginning of the nineteenth centuries, Ashkenazic customs replaced the Sephardic. Especially from the 1880s on, as more than two million Russian-Polish Jews came to the United States, the Ashkenazic ways became the basic Orthodox ways, and hundreds of *shuls*, as the European Jews preferred to call their synagogues, sprung up across the land.

Clearly, Orthodoxy in America was not a new form of Judaism. It was a combination of the three types of European Orthodoxy: Spanish/Portuguese, west European, and east European. And even though these three differed in some ways, such as in their pronunciation of Hebrew, they agreed in their belief in a personal God, in the Torah as Israel's binding guidebook, in *mitzvot* as God's commands, in Sabbath and festivals, in Hebrew prayers traditionally chanted, in the dietary laws, and in the importance of Jewish laws of marriage and divorce. They also believed in following the rules of the Bible, the Talmud, and the *Shulhan Aruch,* the major code of Jewish law.

ORTHODOX PATTERNS

Each of the three waves of immigration added its own special flavor to the life of American Orthodoxy. The Sephardim, for example, patterned their services on the synagogues of London and Amsterdam. They chanted Hebrew with Sephardic tunes and pronounced Hebrew much as Israelis do today. They also stressed decorum or good behavior at worship services. In fact, the early minute books of the six Sephardic congregations that existed at the time of the Revolution tell of fines against worshippers who talked or misbehaved during prayers. They set up religious schools called talmud torahs or yeshivahs in which they taught Jewish studies as well as Spanish, English, mathematics, and other subjects. They also built cemeteries and ritual baths and created charity funds to distribute *tzedakah* to the poor and sick. Before the first Sephardic rabbis came to America, the congregations were led by "ministers" or "reverends" who chanted the services, taught in the religious schools, and like the Christian clergy preached English sermons on Sabbaths and festivals.

These sermons in English were an American innovation. When Reverend Gershom Mendes Seixas of New York and Reverend Isaac Leeser of Philadelphia introduced the sermon to the service, many of the worshippers objected. But the preachers insisted, and the English sermon was finally accepted in Sephardic synagogues. On this question the word of the reverends was taken. But on the questions of Jewish law the ministers had to send to London or Amsterdam for the answer, which might be months in coming.

Since few Sephardic settlers came to America after the eighteenth century, the new Ashkenazic settlers slowly took over the leadership and built their own institutions. This German community wanted its own synagogues and religious leaders and prayer customs. The first such congregation was formed in Easton, Pennsylvania, in 1761. It did not last long. In 1802 the German-Jewish community in Philadelphia created Rodeph Shalom Congre-

Orthodox dignitaries pose on the front steps of the Rabbi Isaac Elchanan Theological Seminary. In a few short years this school became Yeshiva University.

gation, which today is a Reform temple. New York's Dutch and English Jews followed Philadelphia's example and formed B'nai Jeshurun in 1825. It is now a Conservative congregation.

Throughout the 1830s and 1840s new Ashkenazic synagogues were organized all over America while no new Sephardic ones were formed. Some of these Germanic Orthodox synagogues were influenced by the great German Orthodox leader Rabbi Samson Raphael Hirsch. Hirsch led the Frankfort Jewish community and taught that the Torah should be combined with worldly culture. He called upon the Jews to accept the new freedoms they were receiving in Germany and to live outside the ghettos. Hirsch dressed in robes like those of a Protestant minister and unlike his more old-fashioned colleagues he did not wear a full beard. He preached and wrote in German. But he was always faithful to tradition: He insisted on keeping the *mitzvot* with no compromises, and he fought the Reform movement in Germany with all his strength. Hirsch became the hero of modern German Orthodoxy and, as we shall see, his approach to Judaism was eventually accepted by the eastern European Jews who were to become the future leaders of the American Orthodox community.

More than any other influence, it was the massive immigration of eastern European Jews beginning around 1881 that changed the face of American Orthodoxy and American Jewry. Hundreds of shuls were organized; rabbis and cantors, shohetim and mohalim, scribes and scholars arrived and set down roots in New York, Philadelphia, Boston, Chicago, St. Louis, and Los Angeles. In 1880 the eastern European Jews were only 10 percent of the Jewish population in America. By 1906 they were 75 percent, and by 1916 the majority of the nineteen hundred synagogues in America were peopled by east European Jews. Shuls were often named for the immigrants' home towns in Russia or Poland, Hungary or Rumania. New talmud torahs and *heders* (one-room schools), each with its *melamed* (teacher), taught Orthodox customs to the young. Things began to look more hopeful for religious Judaism, and Orthodoxy felt alive in its new homeland.

It was not so simple. Before 1880 the New World was not an easy place for observant Jews. The Jewish population was small, there were no rabbis or professional teachers (before 1840), and there were no good religious schools or yeshivot or seminaries until the end of the nineteenth century. So it was difficult for a Jew to keep kosher or observe the Sabbath.

The diary of one humble, traditional Jewish peddlar recounts how he said his Sabbath prayers, then strapped his pack to his back and set off, with a heavy heart and against his will, to earn a living on a day when it is prohibited to work. But he had no choice: In America it was almost impossible to rest on the Shabbat. In many parts of the land, kosher food was unheard of.

Many Jews married Christians and some even converted away from Judaism. Rabbi Abraham Rice of Baltimore, the first Orthodox rabbi to settle in the United States, wrote to his teacher in Germany: "I dwell in complete isolation without a teacher or a companion in this land whose atmosphere is not conducive to wisdom." Poor Rabbi Rice wondered whether an Orthodox Jew could survive here. Likewise, Rabbi Abraham W. Edelman of Los Angeles struggled to keep his congregation in the ranks of tradition. In the end he failed and was forced to take another post. By 1880 most of the older German synagogues had become either Reform or Conservative, and the outlook seemed hopeless.

Then the eastern European Jews arrived. Many problems still remained. Jews were often forced to work on the Sabbath or on festivals. There was little control over kosher foods and meats, and there was a great deal of fraud and corruption. The quality of the schools was still low and teachers were not well trained. (In New York City in 1910, for example, three-quarters of the children received *no* Jewish education at all; while those who went to school for Jewish training usually attended inferior heders where little was taught.) And, to make things worse, there were simply not enough practicing rabbis and the small congregations could not afford to support rabbis on a full-time salary. In New York City, there were 130 Orthodox shuls on the Lower East Side and only three or four part-time rabbis.

YESHIVA UNIVERSITY— FROM ITS BEGINNINGS

The great immigration of eastern European Jews meant that there were many Orthodox children who needed a good religious education. The lack of rabbis meant that schools were needed to train the youth and prepare boys for the rabbinate. Realizing the terrible lack of good religious schools, a group of devoted laymen formed Etz Chaim Yeshivah on the Lower East Side of New York in 1886. Their purpose was

> the improvement of the spiritual, mental, and social condition of Hebrew boys, to provide for their teaching and instructions in Hebrew, to foster and encourage the study of the Sacred Scriptures, the Talmud, and the Hebrew language and literature, to hold religious services in accordance with Orthodox Judaism: also to provide teachers and instructors for said Hebrew boys in reading, writing, and speaking the English language.

Classes met in a dingy room in New York's Jewish ghetto, and the pupils ranged in age from nine to fifteen. The school grew slowly. Money was a constant problem. And the promise to teach secular subjects was all but forgotten.

In 1897 another center for learning, the Rabbi Isaac Elchanan Theological Seminary, was organized on the Lower East Side. This yeshivah was designed for older boys in order to "promote the study of the Talmud and to assist in educating and preparing students of the Hebrew faith for the Hebrew Orthodox Ministry." The school also taught secular subjects in the afternoon. By 1902 there were more than fifty students enrolled. In 1903 one rabbinical group called the school the only legitimate yeshivah in America. Even so, the school had problems raising money from the very start.

Finally in 1915 the two schools agreed to become one. The success of the combined school was assured by the new president. Rabbi Bernard Revel had come to America from Lithuania in 1906 and was the first scholar to receive a Ph.D. from Dropsie College in Philadelphia. Far and wide he was respected as a great student of Talmud. From the very start, Revel worked to build the small yeshivah into an institution of learning and scholarship. To the original school he added a high school and a Hebrew teachers' college; and in 1928 he founded Yeshiva College, the first Jewish college in the United States. Yeshiva College offered both Jewish and general subjects and gave a course of study leading to rabbinical school. The motto chosen for the school was "Torah and Science." Revel headed the school and its seminary until his death in 1940.

New York's Yeshiva University trains lawyers, doctors, scholars, educators, and Orthodox rabbis.

When Revel died, the leadership passed to Dr. Samuel Belkin. Belkin continued to watch over the growth of Yeshiva College until his death in 1976. Under his guidance it became a full-fledged university with its own medical school, law school, and several graduate divisions. Today, Yeshiva University has over seven thousand students. Its current president is Dr. Norman Lamm, himself a Yeshiva graduate.

Other yeshivot and seminaries followed. Chicago's Orthodox Jewish community set up its Hebrew Theological College in 1921. Over the years it has ordained several hundred rabbis, and today has a junior college for secular studies. Other, less modern yeshivot in Baltimore, Cleveland, New York, and New Jersey grant *semichah* (ordination) to Orthodox rabbinical students. For the most part, these yeshivot do not offer secular studies and do not encourage their students to attend secular colleges. Some of the more traditional yeshivot

A circumcision plate made in Poland in the 1700s, showing the traditional story of the binding of Isaac.

do permit students to take courses in subjects such as mathematics or English, but not in science or philosophy or any subject that might conflict with Orthodox views.

For elementary and high school students there are today more than three hundred yeshivot throughout the country. Over seventy thousand students attend these day schools which are usually administered by Torah Umesorah, the national agency for Orthodox yeshivah education.

ORTHODOXY ORGANIZES

At first many of the eastern European Orthodox leaders believed that Orthodoxy could flourish in America only if it were united. One early attempt was made to form an association of Orthodox synagogues, but it failed. So the leaders turned to another plan. What was needed, they argued, was a chief rabbi who would control all religious and educational affairs. After all, there were chief rabbis in England and France. Why not here, too? So in 1887 Rabbi Jacob Joseph of Vilna was invited to become New York City's first chief rabbi of the Orthodox community. He began the task in 1888 and worked hard to improve the community. But the rabbis already working in New York were jealous and refused to recognize Rabbi Joseph's leadership. Rabbi Joseph died in 1902, a broken and disillusioned man. Jews in other cities tried the same experiment. It failed everywhere. By and large, American Jews have not reacted well to the idea of a central leader or organization that would control their religious lives.

It was not until 1898 that a successful attempt was made to unite the Orthodox synagogues. By this time the Reform movement was growing stronger and was well organized, while the Orthodox felt threatened, divided, and weak. The call for a meeting went out and one thousand delegates gathered at New York's Spanish and Portuguese Synagogue. They voted to establish the Union of Orthodox Jewish Congregations.

Rabbi Henry Pereira Mendes was elected president of the new group, and he was joined by a distinguished group of rabbis and lay leaders. It was clear from the start that this group was "anti-Reform." Its purpose was to "advance the interests of positive Biblical, Rabbinical, Traditional, and Historical Judaism." The leaders called for future gatherings of eminent rabbis and wise laymen to discuss problems of Jewish law. The Union affirmed its belief that

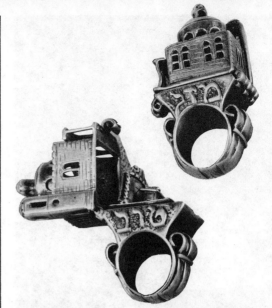

For generations the finest Jewish art has centered around traditional customs and ceremonies. This wedding ring from the early 1800s wishes the new couple a Mazal Tov—"Good Luck."

God had given the Torah and its laws, that the rabbinic interpretations in the Talmud and law codes were binding, and that the Reform views on conversion and intermarriage were totally unacceptable. The platform of the new Union also stated that the Jews are "a nation temporarily without a national home" and that a return to Zion is a basic ideal of Judaism that must not be forsaken.

Gradually the less Orthodox members withdrew from the Union and joined the newly formed Conservative group (organized in 1913). But the Orthodox Union continued to grow. Slowly its members changed from Yiddish-speaking immigrants to English-speaking, American-born Jews. The Union later added a women's division, a youth department called the National Conference of Synagogue Youth, and a college group known as Yavneh which has worked to promote

DIVISIONS WITHIN ORTHODOXY

Preserving the practice of centuries, each Orthodox family prepares for Sukkot by purchasing its own *lulav* and *etrog*.

kashrut (dietary laws) on campus. The Union has also been active in supervising the preparation of kosher foods throughout the country. Its symbol, the U encircled by an O, can be seen on many food products in stores across the country. Today about sixteen hundred Orthodox shuls belong to the Union, representing about 205,640 families.

A number of synagogue groups in Orthodox life have remained separate from the Union because they do not consider the Union to be sufficiently pious. One such independent group is the National Council of Young Israel, founded in 1912. Today it numbers about one hundred synagogues, with more than twenty-five thousand families. Other loose federations of congregations have been organized by the Hasidic and ultra-Orthodox groups. In addition, Sephardic Jews from Turkey, Greece, and Syria who have come to America in the last fifty years have their own synagogue organizations.

THE ORTHODOX RABBINATE

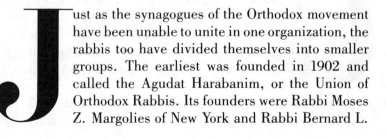

Just as the synagogues of the Orthodox movement have been unable to unite in one organization, the rabbis too have divided themselves into smaller groups. The earliest was founded in 1902 and called the Agudat Harabanim, or the Union of Orthodox Rabbis. Its founders were Rabbi Moses Z. Margolies of New York and Rabbi Bernard L.

Levinthal of Philadelphia. Most of the members of this Union were Yiddish-speaking Orthodox rabbis who had been trained in Europe. The group endorsed the Rabbi Isaac Elchanan Theological Seminary as its official school and attacked the Reform and Conservative groups for not following tradition, particularly in observance of the Sabbath and the dietary laws.

As time passed, the European rabbis disappeared from the scene and the Union of Orthodox Rabbis declined. The younger, American-trained Orthodox rabbis felt a need to organize their own group and in 1935 established the Rabbinical Council of America. At first this group was made up only of the graduates of the seminary. Later on, men who were ordained in other yeshivot were invited to join. By 1977 there were about a thousand members.

In the course of time several other smaller rabbinic associations such as the Rabbinical Alliance and the Hasidic Union of Grand Rabbis were created. But the Rabbinical Council of America is the largest, most powerful, and most representative body of modern Orthodox rabbis in America. Its spiritual leader and most respected scholar is Rabbi Joseph B. Soloveitchik of Boston, who also teaches Talmud and philosophy at Yeshiva University.

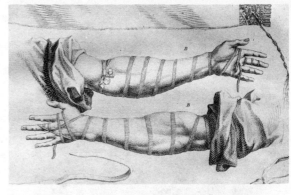

This 18th century etching shows how the leather straps of the tefillin are wound around the arm. Orthodox males wear tefillin on head and arm during morning prayers each weekday.

ORTHODOXY AND ZIONISM

From the start the Orthodox felt that the Zionist movement was irreligious or even antireligious. In 1901 they organized their own Zionist movement, the Mizrachi, to work for a rebuilt religious Jewish state in Israel. Mizrachi sought to develop the idea of a Jewish state run according to the laws and ideals of the Torah. Its women's division and youth group (B'nai Akivah) have been very active here and in Israel. Smaller Orthodox Zionist movements also appeared over the course of the years and recently Mizrachi and these smaller movements

Much of the best Jewish art was created for Passover objects. This Pesah plate contains the *kiddush* prayer and the order (*seder*) of the meal.

were united as the Religious Zionists of America.

Here, too, the ultra-Orthodox, refusing to go along with the liberal majority, formed their own associations. Most of them belong to the Agudat Israel, an international organization of Orthodox Jews. Before 1948 the Agudat Israel bitterly opposed a Jewish state because they thought of the Zionists as nonreligious and because they believed that only the Messiah could rebuild the Holy Land. Since the birth of Israel, however, the Agudat Israel group has supported the state, but is still bitterly critical of Mizrachi and opposes it for not being pious enough. The leaders of America's Agudat Israel are the various heads of the more traditional yeshivot, including both Hasidic and non-Hasidic rabbis. The ultra-Orthodox community, still mainly Yiddish-speaking Jews, looks to these religious leaders as their spokesmen.

Even here, everyone does not follow the same leaders and scholars. The more modern Lubavitcher Rebbe, leader of the largest and most dynamic Hasidic group in America, is constantly criticized by the superpious Satmar Rebbe and his Hasidim who consider the Lubavitcher Rebbe far too liberal. As for the non-Hasidic community, it takes guidance from such sages as the eminent scholar Rabbi Moses Feinstein.

LIGHT AMID SHADOWS

Clearly, the Orthodox community is the least united of all the religious groups in American Jewry. There is no central seminary, no central synagogue group, no single rabbinic association, no single Zionist agency, and no unified platform or creed. Orthodoxy has more shades of opinion today than ever before and it is badly divided.

Despite this division, Orthodoxy in America seems to have come of age. Only seventy years ago it seemed that Orthodoxy could not survive on these shores. As recently as twenty years ago, Orthodoxy was so weak and splintered and the number of Orthodox Jews was shrinking so rapidly that few people gave it more than a generation of life as its future. Yet Orthodoxy is still alive and flourishing. Its yeshivot are crowded, its synagogues are filled with young people, its youth seminars are successful.

Orthodox Jews observe ritual rules such as kashrut, the laws of the Shabbat, and mikveh. True Orthodoxy outside of the large urban centers such as New York or Chicago is almost non-existent. But in the large cities it is the Orthodox synagogues that are usually most crowded with worshippers.

The Hanukkah menorah **celebrates with light the story of the Maccabean struggle for religious freedom. This silver** menorah **made sometime in the 18th century comes from Padua, Italy.**

Thus we could say that Orthodoxy has found a place in the American Jewish scene. Naturally, the European-born ultra-Orthodox still speak Yiddish and live in ghettos, but the majority of modern Orthodox Jews are reasonably involved in the mainstream of Jewish American life.

At the same time, Orthodoxy has become less tolerant of other Jewish groups and less inclined to cooperate with non-Orthodox Jews. Perhaps this separation helps the Orthodox to feel more secure. Perhaps it is because recent yeshivah graduates are less broad-minded and liberal than those of the previous generation. But one thing is certain: The oldest religious group in American Jewish life is alive and dynamic.

At the heart of Orthodoxy is the love of Torah. Studying Bible, Talmud, commentaries, and responsa is a part of daily life—a *mitzvah* observed by young and old.

THE ORTHODOX
IN AMERICA

Torah education never ends. From the day school to the yeshivah, from child to adult, the true Orthodox Jew continues to discuss and read the holy books. Even graduation from college is seen as just one step on the ladder of learning.

THE ORTHODOX IN AMERICA

Most important for the Orthodox Jew is the study of Talmud. In the books of the Talmud is the Oral Law which traditional Jews believe was given by God to Moses; and the great commentaries on the Oral Law such as those of Rashi and his pupils.

Traditionally, the Talmud is studied with a partner, or in small groups. This method is called hevrutah, from the word haver, meaning "friend." But whether in groups or alone, study is seen as a true source of joy.

**THE ORTHODOX
IN AMERICA**

To be a true mitzvah, study must be turned to action. The lighting of the candles in the home brings the family close together at the beginning of Shabbat and other Jewish festivals.

And Jewish law extends beyond
the home life of the Orthodox Jew.
Lending a hand in a senior citizen's
home and inviting the stranger to
share one's Passover meal are
important ways of showing that the
law is not just a set of rules, but a
way of life.

THE ORTHODOX
IN AMERICA

ORTHODOX JUDAISM: BELIEFS AND PRACTICES

Orthodox Judaism, by and large, is not deeply concerned with philosophy, ideology, or beliefs. It seems to agree with the old rabbinic statement "The idea is not as important as the deed." Consequently, few Orthodox rabbis or thinkers have written on philosophical ideas. Most prefer to deal with matters of Jewish law they consider to be basic. They are content to follow medieval thinkers' ideas about God, Torah, sin, humanity, the Jewish people, and the World to Come. And just about all Orthodox thinkers today define Judaism as a "religion" based on a legal order or system *(halachah)* that governs the behavior of a Jew from sunrise to sunset, from birth to death.

The Orthodox consider themselves to be the only true Jews. They feel that the other movements (Conservative, Reform, Reconstructionist, secularist, and Zionist) are betrayals of God's laws and violations of the Torah; and as such are mistaken, sinful, or worse and soon will disappear.

BELIEFS ABOUT GOD

Orthodoxy accepts the traditional views of God as developed in the Bible, Talmud, and Midrash and as taught in the writings of medieval philosophers. To an Orthodox Jew, God is a spirit in the universe that has created all things and keeps all things alive. God is all-powerful, all-knowing, all-wise, and universal. God sees our actions; hears our thoughts, prayers, and words; God is aware of all we say and do. People understand God's will by studying Torah and performing mitzvot, the commandments.

Every Jew is required to hear the blowing of the *shofar* on the High Holy Days.

Believing that God is all-powerful and totally in control gives rise to a difficult question: Why is there evil in the world? In our times this question has taken on a new meaning, and modern Jewish thinkers have asked, "Why did the Holocaust take place; and where was God when six million Jews were sent to their deaths?" Not many Orthodox thinkers have dared to deal with this subject. One who has, Rabbi Eliezer Berkovits, admits that we simply cannot know the purpose behind the Holocaust. We certainly cannot think that all the Jews were slaughtered because they were sinners. To believe that would be to think of God as unspeakably cruel. But even though we as human beings cannot understand God's purpose in the Holocaust, we can take comfort in knowing that the state of Israel was born out of that tragedy.

TORAH

One subject that Orthodox thinkers take seriously is the question of Torah and the Torah's place in Jewish life. It is an Orthodox belief that the Torah is the revealed word of God, given at Mount Sinai thirty-one centuries ago. To be Orthodox, a Jew must be "Torah-true" and must believe that every word, every law, every commandment of the Bible as explained and developed by the rabbis is God's word and thus is binding on a loyal Jew. Most Orthodox thinkers insist that the words of the written Torah *and* the oral laws and interpretations are God's words, and are of equal importance. The 613 mitzvot found in the Torah are all of *equal* importance, and no human has the right to choose one over another. Furthermore, the ritual laws (such as kashrut) and the ethical laws (such as love of neighbor) are equally vital, and a Torah-true Jew is expected to practice both kinds.

Once this basic understanding of the Torah's place is accepted, it is not difficult for a person to be an Orthodox Jew. For, if the Bible is God's word rather than the word of human beings, how can we *not* keep its laws? And once we agree that the rabbinic interpretations of those laws are true for all time, then those laws must be observed as well. This is the Orthodox view of halachah.

Many Orthodox thinkers have spent entire lifetimes exploring the idea of halachah, Jewish law. Rabbi Joseph B. Soloveitchik has called upon every Jew to become an ish halachah, a person of the law. He believes that the importance of halachah does not have to be proved because the law comes from God. By controlling our emotions and instincts, halachah brings us closer to God; it sets up rules that cannot be broken by our own will or our desires or our emotions. Rabbi Soloveitchik points out that halachah is concerned with every discovery and every insight into humanity and the world around us, even to the exploration of outer space and scientific experimentation on our own planet. The purpose of halachah, Rabbi Soloveitchik concludes, is to unite our creative role in the universe with God's creative force.

Other Orthodox writers have seen other purposes for the law. The late Rabbi Samuel Belkin, for example, noted that all mitzvot have a higher moral purpose, even when we cannot understand it. Even something as simple as not eating shellfish can be morally important in a way which we may never know.

Rabbi Emanuel Rackman suggests that the laws prohibiting work on the Sabbath and festivals are designed to teach us not to exploit nature—at least on special days. On these holy days we are in harmony with nature.

The Torah can be wrapped in a mantle and decorated with a crown and shield in the Western style; or encased in the Sephardic style seen here. When this Torah is being read, its case is open and it stands upright on the reading desk.

Rabbi Eliezer Berkovits thinks that the halachah educates us, teaches us to be less self-centered, helps us to control our appetites and instincts, and shows us the way to help others while binding ourselves to God.

The stricter, ultra-Orthodox rabbis do not like these explanations of halachah; they believe that it is enough to know that the laws are the will of

God. Knowing that, the pious Jew must cherish and keep the laws—without questioning or reasoning.

But can the laws be changed, or are the mitzvot to remain the same for all times? The ultra-Orthodox insist that the laws can never be changed. They may sometimes be given new explanations or interpretations, but these explanations can come only from the *gedolay hador,* the great sages and yeshivah heads of the times. By contrast, the more liberal thinkers among the Orthodox believe that the rabbis do have some leeway in offering new explanations or finding loopholes so that laws may be changed even if "unofficially." Rabbi Leo Jung, for example, argues that an Orthodox *bet din* (court of law, usually made up of rabbis) has the power to pass emergency laws and find new interpretations for new situations. Many others, including Rabbi Rackman, suggest that Orthodox rabbis are too often lost in their studies and out of touch with real life. If Orthodox rabbis are to solve human problems, they must feel the way their followers feel and understand the way their congregants must live and the world in which they live.

In the same way, Rabbi Berkovits is sharply critical of Orthodox scholars who close themselves in "ivory towers" and neglect the real needs of the people. Berkovits argues that Jewish law has changed and developed through the course of our history, that some laws were dropped for ethical or even economic reasons while new laws were added to meet new needs. He urges that the Orthodox return to "authentic Judaism" by dealing honestly and bravely with current problems such as women's rights, birth control, and autopsy. In fact, Berkovits is one of the very few bold Orthodox spokesmen for equal treatment of women.

It is obvious that Orthodox rabbis and scholars, while firmly believing in halachah, approach it in many ways. The ultra-Orthodox seem content to leave things as they are. The liberals urge change and growth, but only under the guidance of rabbis and scholars. Even the most eminent authorities, such as Israel's two chief rabbis, Shlomo Goren and Ovadiah Yoseph, have given opposing legal rulings.

The same is true in America where the Lubavitcher Rebbe and Rabbi Moses Feinstein disagree sharply on issues such as birth control. No doubt the main reason for these differences of opinion is that there is no one central rabbinical organization or law committee or *sanhedrin* (high court) in Orthodox life today.

Still, despite differences in approach or opinion, one thing remains constant: All Orthodox rabbis and scholars and, theoretically, all Orthodox Jewish men and women accept halachah, Jewish law, as their constitution for Jewish living and as God's word.

O rthodox Jews believe in the ancient idea that Jews are the chosen people of God. There are many prayers in the daily, Sabbath, and festival worship services that express this belief. One of the most common is the prayer a person recites upon receiving an *aliyah,* the honor of being called to the Torah, in which we thank God "who chose us from all other peoples." Some have understood these words to mean that Jews are better than non-Jews. Most, however, believe this prayer implies that Jews must be a holy nation and a Kingdom of Priests, a "light to the nations," and that Jews must serve God, study and teach God's Torah, spread God's word to the nations of the world, and live up to a higher standard of ethics and morality, of ritual and practice. Whether most Orthodox Jews live up to this concept of the chosen people is hard to measure. But all do accept the idea, and no Orthodox rabbi or scholar would suggest removing the chosen people concept from the prayers.

THE JEWISH PEOPLE

E *retz Yisrael,* the Land of Israel, is and always has been precious to the Jewish people. Orthodox Jews revere Israel as the Holy Land. Almost all Orthodox Jews hope that the modern state of Israel will be run according to the principles of the Torah and that halachah might set the guiding rules of the state. But there is a definite split in Orthodox ranks over the meaning of the state of Israel.

THE LAND OF ISRAEL

On one side is the ultra-Orthodox minority which is uncomfortable with the new state and the government of Israel. While they pray fervently for and cherish the idea of Eretz Yisrael, they do not believe that secular or nonreligious Jews have the right to set up a Jewish state, and they insist that only the Messiah, the supernatural Redeemer to be sent by God, can accomplish that task. The ultra-Orthodox trust that God, when ready, will establish the Jewish nation based on the Torah in the Holy Land. All attempts to achieve that goal now are premature and possibly even sinful. Because of this belief,

Jews who keep the laws of kashrut have a special set of dishes for Passover. Whenever possible, each member of the family is given a beautifully decorated haggadah from which to read; and the kiddush cup and seder plate may be true objects of art.

some of the ultra-Orthodox will not even recognize the state of Israel and go so far as to reject it publicly.

But the majority of Orthodox Jews, the liberals, are thrilled that the state has been reborn. Many have gone to settle there since 1948, and American Orthodox Jews have established yeshivot, schools (including Bar-Ilan University), health facilities, and housing developments in Israel. Orthodox Jews of the Mizrachi Zionist movement look to Israel's chief rabbis for religious guidance.

Here in America and in Israel, the Orthodox constantly press for the state to follow the Torah and mitzvot. Rabbi Soloveitchik, for example, considers Israel to be a means to a higher end. In his view, Israel should be the fulfillment of the destiny of the community of Torah people. The Lubavitcher Rebbe states that to be a Jewish state, Israel must be run according to the Messianic tradition—"in accordance with the laws of the Torah"—for Israel is *the* Holy Land and a special place. The Rebbe has expressed his fears that because Israel is officially a secular state, its new generation will grow up divorced from the past of the Jewish people and cut off from its eternal values.

Orthodox Jews urge that the Torah must form at least part of the constitution of the state of Israel, that Sabbath and dietary rules be enforced, that no public transportation run on the Sabbath and holy days, that only marriages conducted by Orthodox rabbis be recognized, and that religion be part of the national educational system. Orthodox Jews have generally opposed the growth of non-Orthodox religious movements in Israel and have denounced Conservative and Reform rabbis who have tried to establish liberal synagogues in various communities in the new state.

THE JEWISH COMMUNITY

The ultra-Orthodox minority has avoided working with non-Orthodox groups as much as possible. There are several reasons for this lack of cooperation. First, the ultra-Orthodox consider the non-Orthodox Jews to be heretics and non-believers who should be avoided and cut off from the community. Second, they believe that working together with the non-Orthodox would mean recognizing the right of non-Orthodox groups to exist. And, too, they fear that since the Orthodox are such a small minority they would be outvoted and overpowered by the majority and their positions would be undermined or ignored.

For these reasons, some of the leading Orthodox sages (including the Lubavitcher Rebbe) have prohibited their followers from joining umbrella groups such as the New York Board of Rabbis and the Synagogue Council of America since non-Orthodox rabbis and laypeople belong to these organizations.

But just as the Orthodox world seems split on every other issue, here too the liberal Orthodox majority has tried to cooperate with their non-Orthodox Jewish neighbors as best as possible. They have been active in community groups such as the rabbinical boards, the Synagogue Council of America, Federation of Jewish Philanthropies, United Jewish Appeal; and they have worked with the non-Orthodox community in support of Israel and Soviet Jewry. But when it comes to matters of Jewish law or ritual observances, even the liberal Orthodox draw the line on cooperation.

Of late even the liberal Orthodox have been less anxious to work together with other movements, since many of the joint activities do involve matters of law and ritual. This may be the beginning of a new mood of separatism for American Orthodoxy. Few Orthodox rabbis or laypeople have concerned themselves with economic, social, and political problems that affect the general community such as civil rights and international affairs. One reason for this lack of interest is that, until recently, the Orthodox themselves did not feel quite at home in America. Also, they prefer to concentrate on purely Jewish matters such as Torah education, kashrut, and halachah.

Of course, the Orthodox have taken up matters of vital concern to their own community. For example, they continually fight against laws that might destroy the right of the Jewish community to buy kosher-slaughtered meat. And they fight to protect the rights of Sabbath-observers. In the last few years they have campaigned to receive federal and state funding to help their yeshivot, many of which are deeply in debt.

Some of the more progressive Orthodox rabbis are disappointed that

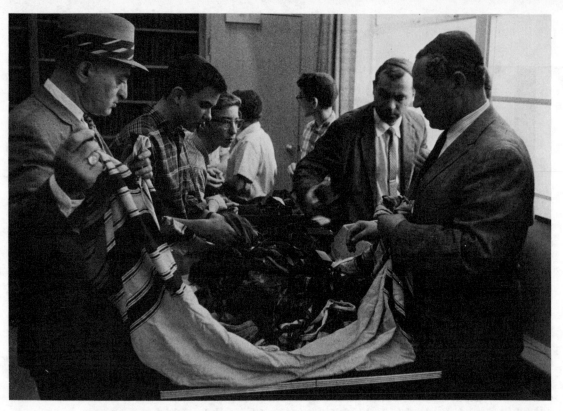

Books which contain the name of God, and religious objects which either contain God's name or have been used in worship, are not destroyed. They are carefully gathered and buried with full ceremony. Their burial place is called a genizah, and in some ways it serves as a kind of time capsule which future generations may discover (as we have discovered ancient genizah sites) and study.

Orthodox Jews have not been sufficiently involved in the social issues that the Jewish community in America faces. Rabbi Leo Jung, for instance, accuses his fellow Orthodox rabbis of having neglected the social-righteousness programs of the Torah and the Torah's proposals for solving the ills of society. Rabbi Emanuel Rackman has issued a similar plea for Orthodox Jews to care about the needs of other peoples and to turn their attention to the pressing problems of modern society. But for the moment these pleas have largely gone unheard.

Most Orthodox rabbis are opposed to dialogue with Christian clergy. They see such discussion and debate as foolish and fruitless, and they fear that such occasions will turn into missionary campaigns aimed at converting Jews to Christianity. Rabbi Soloveitchik has suggested a middle path, saying that it is proper for Jews and non-Jews to work together in secular areas of concern, but it is absurd to try to cooperate in theological or religious matters since differences between Christianity and Judaism are too great to be ignored or overcome. He adds the caution that dialogue and common work can be shared only so long as Christians accept Jews as equals and do not seek to blame the Jews for the death of Jesus.

INTERFAITH ACTIVITIES

Orthodox Judaism is an all-encompassing system of commandments laid down in the Bible and Talmud and spelled out in the *Shulhan Aruch*, the Code of Jewish Law. A truly Orthodox Jew observes mitzvot from the the moment of awakening in the morning to the moment of falling asleep at night.

RELIGIOUS PRACTICES

Following mitzvot strictly is basic to Orthodox Jewish life. The Orthodox male must be circumcised according to law by a *mohel*. The female is named in the synagogue, usually on the first Sabbath after her birth. Children are to receive a good, intensive Jewish education, preferably in a yeshivah or day school where religious subjects are emphasized over secular subjects. At age thirteen, a Jewish boy becomes *Bar Mitzvah* in the synagogue. Orthodox girls rarely receive official recognition or *Bat Mitzvah*. An Orthodox boy or girl is expected to marry within the faith according to the Jewish laws of matrimony and with a rabbi conducting the ceremony. Orthodox Jews consider mixed marriage (marriage to a non-Jew) a sin, and they will not accept converts where the purpose of the conversion is marriage. If the marriage fails, the partners must receive a Jewish divorce, or *get*. An Orthodox rabbi will never remarry a Jew who was once married and lacks a get. When an Orthodox Jew dies, the body is prepared for burial according to Jewish law by being washed and dressed in plain linen wrappings by a special Holy Burial Society, then placed in a simple coffin. Mourners tear their garments as a sign of grief (this is called *keriah*), observe seven days of mourning during which they do no work (the seven-day period is called *shivah*, from the Hebrew word for "seven"), and go to no entertainments. They recite the *Kaddish* prayer daily for eleven months if the deceased is a parent or thirty days for other relatives or for a mate.

Affixed to the doorposts of every Orthodox Jewish home is a *mezuzah*, a small box containing passages from the Torah, to remind the family that the home must be filled with Jewishness. Males cover their heads at all times with a skull cap (in Yiddish, *yarmulke*; in Hebrew, *kippah*) or hat as a sign of respect for God; married women cover their hair with a kerchief or wig as a sign of modesty. Men are required to pray three times daily and wear a prayer shawl (*talit*) and phylacteries (*tefillin*) each morning. Every Orthodox Jew tries to study the Torah daily. Orthodox Jews eat only kosher food, never mix milk and meat, are careful not to eat bread or other products prepared with leavening during Passover, and recite a blessing before and after each meal. The Orthodox woman is expected to maintain a kosher home, light Sabbath and festival candles, and go to the ritual bath (*mikveh*) after each menstrual period.

The Orthodox are careful to observe the Sabbath and festivals in every way. They will not work, write, smoke, ride, or carry even a handkerchief out of their homes on the Sabbath, nor will they use radio, television, or lights on that day. They build a *sukkah* at home on the festival of Sukkot, fast on Yom Kippur and other holy fast days, eat only foods that are kosher for *Pesah* during Passover, and observe all the other rituals for each holy day of the year.

Orthodox Jews will pray only in an Orthodox shul. The shul is designed so that men and women sit separately with a partition or curtain (*mehitzah*) between them so that they will not distract members of the opposite sex. The service is almost entirely in Hebrew, although the more modern synagogues have added some English prayers and an English sermon by the rabbi. The traditional prayerbook (*Siddur*) is the only one used, and no changes or additions to the prayers are allowed. Musical instruments and choirs with female singers are never allowed at Sabbath or holy day services.

The Orthodox are strict about not changing the prayer services or any of the prayers. They believe that those who have altered these things have often adopted Christian ways such as mixed seating, organs, and mixed choirs, and that these are signs of assimilation. They feel that the traditional prayers are beautiful as they stand and that it is arrogant and improper to change them. And even if they do not totally accept certain ideas in the Siddur such as the resurrection of the dead or Heaven and Hell, they are not prepared to drop these ideas.

In other ways, however, some modern Orthodox congregations have adopted new patterns. They have sometimes become synagogue-centers with clubs, youth programs, and athletic activities; and most Orthodox rabbis preach in English on subjects of current interest. In every other respect, Orthodox services today are almost the same as they were in Europe a century ago.

Women have almost no role in synagogue worship in the Orthodox movement, and while most seem content with this, some women have been asking for greater opportunities to participate in worship. As a result, some Orthodox shuls have created a sort of Bat Mitzvah ceremony for girls even though this is a change in tradition. Women have also made demands in other areas of Jewish life. For example, under traditional law a woman cannot inherit if there are males in the family, nor can she be a witness in a court case. And there is a law that says that women cannot issue divorces but can only hope that the men will agree to issue a get. Some Orthodox women want these laws changed. And while few changes have taken place thus far, the winds of women's liberation are blowing in Orthodox Judaism as they are in all religions.

Finally, the Orthodox Jew is expected to conduct his business and professional life according to Jewish law and ethics. In fact, one of the four sections of the *Shulhan Aruch* is concerned with business practice. Truly pious Jews must not cheat or steal or lie; their word must be their bond. They may not lend money at interest; they must pay workers on time; they may not cheat a boss; they must not short-change a customer or give false weight of goods; they must give charity to the poor and help the sick and aged. While most Orthodox Jews do respect these ethical laws, others stress the ritual commandments and neglect the ethical. But Orthodoxy does demand that a Jew observe *all* mitzvot equally and so it teaches that ethical rules are always as important as rituals.

The life of an Orthodox Jew is a demanding one and requires great commitment and sacrifice. The essence of Orthodox Judaism is observance of the mitzvot, and the truly Orthodox Jew devotes a lifetime to the service of God, the study of the Torah, and the keeping of God's law.

REFORM JUDAISM

THE MOVEMENT FOR JEWISH REFORM

The roots of Reform Judaism come from the beginning of the modern age in Germany. Following the French Revolution and the Napoleonic Wars, Jews in much of western Europe were given new freedoms. They were suddenly released from the ghettos in which they had been living. In France, Germany, Italy, and Holland they were given the right to vote and other civil liberties. In many places they could enter universities, work at almost any job they chose, even accept public office.

GERMAN BEGINNINGS

But they were hardly ready for this to happen. After living in the darkness of the ghettos for so long, the new freedoms were like a blinding light. Many were confused even as they were excited. For a goodly number, Judaism suddenly seemed old-fashioned, out-of-date. Some of these Jews, looking at the world with their new eyes, moved further and further away from their Judaism. They assimilated, even converted to Christianity.

Others tried to change Judaism to meet the needs of the new life they were living. Reform Judaism was born in this effort and in the hope that changes would stop the terrible wave of assimilation and conversion that was stealing hundreds of Jews away from their faith.

At first no one knew that Reform would be a movement. Individual synagogues, such as the ones in Seesen, Hamburg, and Berlin, trying to modernize Judaism and update religious worship, made changes in their own services and teachings. They introduced prayers and sermons in the German language, used choirs and organ music during services, changed traditional prayers. They wanted to make their synagogues more attractive so that Jews would not be drawn to Protestant or Catholic churches.

As more and more synagogues in western Europe began to make similar changes, there was a need for the new leaders to meet and share their ideas. To meet this need, several rabbinical conferences of reformers were held between 1844 and 1871. At these conferences the leaders tried to work out exactly what this new reform of Judaism should mean and how it should be accomplished. And the reformers found that they shared some basic ideas. Judaism for these leaders was seen as a developing, evolving religion, one that would disappear if it were not kept up-to-date, one which needed constant reform and change.

Mitzvot and customs, such as kashrut, strict Sabbath and festival observance, and the use of Hebrew alone for prayer, were changed or abandoned. And the movement of Reform

Beth Elohim, Charleston's first synagogue, was built in 1795. The Reformers broke away from it in 1824; but in 1836 it became a Reform synagogue.

was born. But it was not in Germany that it would grow and prosper, it was in the New World.

EARLY AMERICAN REFORM

America was ready for Reform and the American Jewish community was eager for it. Unlike Europe, America had no organized Jewish community. Each Jew really could act independently, and did. America was still wilderness and frontier. The pioneering spirit was strong and people felt free to experiment in everything, including religion. There were no national organizations of synagogues, so each congregation was free to make whatever changes and rules it wished. And the liberal spirit of America encouraged freedom of religious expression. It was the perfect soil in which Reform Judaism could grow.

The first Reform congregation was in Charleston, South Carolina. It was formed in 1824 when a group of forty-seven worshippers, led by Isaac Harby and David Carvalho, asked the leaders of Beth Elohim Congregation for a shorter, more orderly service with an English sermon. When the leaders of Beth Elohim refused to make these changes, the reformers broke away and organized the Reformed Society of Israelites. In 1836 the leaders of Beth Elohim finally changed their minds and Beth Elohim became a Reform synagogue, calling upon a new minister, Reverend Gustave Poznanski. Poznanski introduced an organ, preached in English, did away with the second day of the festivals, and shortened the worship services. He proclaimed: "This synagogue is our *temple,* this city our Jerusalem, this happy land our *Palestine.*"

From this beginning, Reform societies and temples spread quickly. Baltimore established its first Reform temple in 1842. New York's Congregation Emanuel followed in 1845. Then Albany, Cincinnati, Philadelphia, Chicago, and other cities joined the movement.

Reform rabbis were imported from Germany, Bohemia, and Austria to lead the new congregations. Each tried to teach his own brand of Reform; each struggled to "modernize" the Jewish religion and update the prayer service.

ISAAC MAYER WISE

Far and away the most important of these immigrant rabbis was Isaac Mayer Wise. He was born in Bohemia in 1819 and came to the United States in 1846. By 1900, the year of his death, he had shaped Reform into a true movement.

Wise first settled in Albany, New York, where he tried to introduce reforms in the synagogue worship. But he was met by strong opposition from the leaders of Albany's synagogue. Seeing that Albany was not ready for the changes he wanted to introduce, Wise moved to Cincinnati in 1854. From Cincinnati, he directed the progress of American Reform Judaism for almost four decades and single-handedly created a progressive movement.

But his master plan was even larger. At first, Wise wished to unite all American synagogues in one organization. In 1873 he established the Union of American Hebrew Congregations. The purpose of the Union was to create a college for rabbis in the United States, to set up religious schools, to aid and encourage new congregations, and to produce textbooks and literature on Jewish subjects. The first twenty-eight congregations to join included some traditional synagogues and so the Union did not seek to make any radical changes at first. Later, as changes were made, some of the more traditional synagogues left the Union. But the Union grew, and by 1880 almost two hundred synagogues were members. In 1905 an education department was added. The Sisterhoods were organized in 1913 and in 1923 a division was set up for Brotherhoods. Later, in 1939, the Union added its youth department, the National Federation of Temple Youth. The greatest period of growth for the Union followed World War II, and today there are more than seven hundred congregations with close to one million members in America alone.

Isaac Mayer Wise (1819-1900) was the first to truly organize American Judaism. Today all movements follow the patterns he set for the Reform movement in America.

REFORM RABBINICAL SCHOOLS

After forming the Union of American Hebrew Congregations, Wise turned to the second step in his plan and set out to organize a college for the training of rabbis and teachers. He had unsuccessfully tried to do this in 1854. But in 1873 a friend from Indiana donated $10,000 to start a new seminary, and the new Union pledged to raise another $60,000. Not only the liberal rabbis supported this project, but several of the traditional rabbis such as Sabato Morais and Benjamin Szold also were in favor of having a seminary.

In 1875 Wise opened the Hebrew Union College in his own synagogue in Cincinnati. There were seventeen students and four instructors. In 1883, after a long and difficult struggle, the first four rabbis were ordained. The celebration would have been complete and Wise's plan to unite American Jewry might even have succeeded, but at the banquet a terrible error was made. Nonkosher food was served. Immediately, Szold, Morais, and the other traditionalists walked out, furious, and the Union was split forever.

The college prospered despite this. Although it did not train *all* American rabbis, as Wise had hoped, it continues to train Reform rabbis even now. After Wise's death, his place as president of the Hebrew Union College was taken by Moses Mielziner, then Kaufmann Kohler, Julian Morgenstern, Nelson Glueck, and in 1971, Alfred Gottschalk. A Hebrew Teachers College was added in 1909 and a School of Sacred Music for the training of cantors in 1948. More recently, a branch of the college was opened in Los Angeles and a School for Archaeology established in Jerusalem. Since its beginning, the college has trained more than one thousand men and women for the Reform rabbinate.

In 1922 another great Reform leader, Rabbi Stephen S. Wise, decided to establish a second Reform seminary.

He was displeased with the Hebrew Union College, feeling that it was too radical and was out of touch with the masses of Jews, especially the new immigrants who had come to America since 1881. He particularly despised the College's anti-Zionist position, feeling that Zionism was an important part of Judaism. He also felt strongly that New York, which had become the true center of Jewish life in America, should have its own seminary. Like Isaac Mayer Wise, Stephen Wise hoped that his school would train students to become rabbis in all branches of Judaism. And with these goals in mind, he set up the Jewish Institute of Religion. He was the president of the Institute until 1948 when the Jewish Institute of Religion merged with the Hebrew Union College which had finally accepted Stephen Wise's views on the importance of Zionism and other critical matters.

UNITING THE RABBIS

The third step in Isaac Mayer Wise's grand design was to unite all America's rabbis into one group. It was perhaps the most difficult of all the tasks he had chosen. Many of his personal views were not acceptable to the more traditional rabbis, and in order to create a single organization he had to compromise many of these views for the sake of peace and harmony. Finally a group was formed in 1855. However, after a few years, it fell apart.

Wise tried again in 1869. Although Wise was now considered to be a moderate reformer and the more traditional rabbis were willing to accept him as a leader, a group of radical reformers led by the brilliant Kaufmann Kohler demanded that the new group stand for a platform of change. Under Kohler's leadership, the conference proclaimed that they no longer believed in a personal Messiah or in the return of the Jewish people to Zion. They went even

Stephen S. Wise (1874-1949), Reform rabbi, Zionist leader, noted writer, and lecturer. He founded the Jewish Institute of Religion, the American Jewish Congress, and the Free Synagogue of New York.

Bene Yeshurun Temple in Cincinnati. It was here that Isaac Mayer Wise taught and preached; and here that the first class of Hebrew Union College met.

further by declaring that since Hebrew was no longer understood by the majority of the Jews, it could be replaced in the prayer service by English; and they dropped the requirement of a *ketubah* (marriage contract) and a *get* (Jewish divorce). These positions made it all but impossible for any traditional rabbi to belong to the conference.

At a major convention in Pittsburgh in 1885, the conference declared that it was time to reform American Judaism. An eight-point program was adopted by a board of fifteen rabbis which set the tone for Reform Judaism for the next fifty years. The eight points were:

1. Judaism teaches the highest idea of God of any religion because it preaches ethical monotheism.

2. The Bible is the record of Israel's consecration to God.

3. Modern scientific and philosophical ideas are not opposed to Judaism since the teachings of the Bible merely reflect the primitive ideas of the time.

4. Only the moral laws of Judaism are binding. The ritual laws such as kashrut, priestly purity, and dress codes are of pagan origin and are no longer necessary to our spiritual upliftment.

5. We are no longer a nation, but a "religious community," and we no longer expect to return to Palestine or a Jewish state or offer sacrifices in a Temple.

6. Judaism must work with Christianity and Islam to bring truth and righteousness to mankind.

7. The notions of Heaven and Hell and bodily resurrection of the dead are no longer meaningful.

8. Jews must participate in the task of solving the problems of society through a program of social justice.

These eight points were so revolutionary that the traditionalists who remained split with Wise and his group forever. Now there was no chance for creating a single organization to include all American rabbis, but Wise did succeed in joining the Reform rabbis together in one association called the Central Conference of American Rabbis, founded in 1889. Almost a hundred men attended the first conference of this new organization in Detroit, and they chose Isaac Mayer Wise as their first president. Today, the Central Conference of American Rabbis is still the only Reform rabbinical group in America, and its membership is about a thousand men and women. Three of Wise's fondest dreams had come true.

REFORM JUDAISM EXPANDS

Reform Judaism had its greatest early success among German Jewish immigrants in the American South and West. The farther Jews moved away from the major centers of Jewish life, the more accepting they were of radical Reform. But the Reform movement did not attract the large numbers of eastern European Jews who came to America between 1881 and 1914. These Jews were reluctant to join synagogues in which little Hebrew was used, in which men wore no head coverings and sat together with women during prayer services, and in which organs and choirs were a part of the service. Furthermore, the German Jews who belonged to Reform synagogues tended to look down at many of the immigrants since they spoke only Yiddish and had little secular knowledge.

Because the eastern European Jews came from traditional and Orthodox backgrounds they were particularly bothered by the fact that the Reformers did not observe such basic laws as kashrut, they rode to synagogue on the Sabbath, observed only one day of the festivals instead of the traditional two days, and had dropped such rituals as the wearing of talit and tefillin entirely. The Orthodox accused the Reform of imitating the Christians in their use of the organ, in their English-language prayers, and in their not wearing yarmulkes. The Reform replied that the Orthodox were medieval ghetto Jews who fanatically refused to update Judaism and to keep in step with modern times.

Temple Emanu-El of New York, a national landmark of Reform Judaism. Its main sanctuary seats more than 2,000 people.

In the midst of this division, the Reform broke with tradition even more, becoming even more extreme. In 1892 the Central Conference of American Rabbis ruled that circumcision would no longer be required when a male converted to Judaism. Many Reform rabbis instituted Sunday services to replace or supplement the Sabbath services which were hardly attended. Others held a late service on Friday evening in place of the traditional Saturday morning service. In 1897 Wise and his colleagues ruled that the Talmud and the classic texts were no longer binding on Jews. The Reform rabbis sharply attacked Theodor Herzl and the newly formed Zionist movement because they believed that Jews must carry on their mission to the world *outside* of Israel; to do otherwise, they feared, would be disloyal to America. Naturally, as the Reform moved ever farther from tradition, the gap between the movement and the more traditional Jewish community widened.

Meanwhile, the Reform movement strengthened its institutions. The Hebrew Union College built a beautiful Cincinnati campus. The Union of American Hebrew Congregations expanded its programs and helped to publish the *Union Prayer Book* and a variety of textbooks. In 1926 the American Reform movement joined with German and English Reform and created the World Union for Progressive Judaism. This new Union planned to spread the knowledge of God and Reform Judaism throughout the world and to help develop new Reform congregations wherever Jews might be. For a while the main office of the World Union was in New York, but recently it has been moved to Jerusalem. It now services more than a dozen Reform groups in Israel and Reform temples in twenty-four other countries throughout the world.

After World War II, as a part of the renewed interest in religion, Reform went through a new period of growth. Hundreds of Reform temples appeared in suburban areas near New York, Chicago, Los Angeles, Miami, and almost every other large Jewish community in the United States. Under the able leadership of the late Rabbi Maurice Eisendrath, then president of the Union of American Hebrew Congregations, the Reform movement has gained world renown. And while in the last few years the rate of growth has slowed, it is a powerful, well-organized, and basically healthy and dynamic movement.

Reform Judaism was founded on the belief that change in Jewish life is essential and that Judaism must never become fixed or paralyzed. This willingness to change has been so true of the American Reform movement that the movement today is remarkably different from what it was a hundred or even fifty years ago. For example, Reform rabbis who had opposed Zionism in the 1890s gradually shifted to support of the settlement of Jews in Palestine, and eventually, after 1948, became full-fledged supporters of the new nation of Israel. In 1978 the American Reform Zionist Association (ARZA) was founded to represent the Reform movement in the World Zionist Congress.

Over the course of the years, the old opposition to mitzvot disappeared and more and more rabbis and congregations began to restore certain discarded practices such as the use of Hebrew prayers, traditional Sabbath observances, even skull caps and prayer shawls. Various guides to Jewish observance were published for the Reform movement. Reform Sunday schools were enriched and supplemented by additional hours of classes. The 1976 Union prayer book, *The Gates of Prayer,* the 1977 Union prayer book for home worship, *The Gates of the House,* and the 1978 Union prayer book for the high holy days, *The Gates of Repentance*, are all largely in Hebrew and have restored many of the services and traditional prayers that had been removed.

But it was the historic Columbus Platform of 1937 that really marked the end of the older, "classical" Reform movement, and the birth of the new, more traditionally oriented movement. Some of the precepts of the Columbus Platform — it was adopted in Columbus, Ohio — undid many of the precepts of the 1885 Pittsburgh Platform. While the new platform endorsed the idea expressed in Pittsburgh that Judaism is the "historical religious experience of the Jewish people" whose teachings have always developed and changed, it also recognized the need to make the Torah "the dynamic source of the life of Israel," though it called for new interpretations of the Torah for our time.

The Columbus Platform urged Jews to strengthen the Jewish people and rebuild the Land of Israel as a Jewish homeland, a refuge for the oppressed, and a "center of Jewish culture and spiritual life." It spelled out the need to work for social justice, racial brotherhood, and world peace. But its final section was an especially bold change from the old position of Reform because it urged the development of synagogue and home rituals, home prayer, and the use of concrete symbols such as Sabbath and festival observance, mitzvot, and the Hebrew language.

The Reform movement placed great stress on modernizing Jewish art and architecture. This very modern synagogue interior belongs to North Shore Congregation Israel in Glencoe, Illinois.

Ever since 1937 Reform has been finding its way back to more traditional Judaism. Today's Reform services and patterns of observance are different in many ways from those of fifty years ago, and the old hatred of Reform Jews toward the Orthodox is almost nonexistent.

Why did Reform change so sharply? One reason is that it reacted to the changing moods of the times. In the late nineteenth century, rationalism (the belief in our ability to reason) was popular and mysticism and romanticism were out of fashion. So anything that seemed old-fashioned (such as a yarmulke or talit) was denounced as "oriental" and dropped. But with the entry of many eastern European and more traditional Jews into the Reform movement, the fashion changed. These new members had strong ties to tradition and traditional rituals, to Zion and to mitzvot. They wanted a more traditional type of service in their temples than the previous generation had wanted. And the rabbis, who no longer came from German backgrounds, but who were themselves often eastern European immigrants or children of these immigrants, also held on to their deep feelings for tradition. The impact of the new Conservative and Reconstructionist movements was felt in Reform too, causing the Reform leaders to embrace the notion of Peoplehood and a renewed love for Israel. Certainly, too, the Holocaust in Europe and the rebirth of Israel as a nation made a deep impression on Reform and its attitudes.

THE CENTENARY PERSPECTIVE

On the one-hundredth anniversary of the founding of the Hebrew Union College, the Reform movement issued a new statement of principles called the Centenary Perspective. This new platform affirms the belief that the Jewish people is a unique people bound together by language, land, history, culture, and institutions, and inspired by its involvement with God. Judaism emphasizes deed rather than creed as the most important expression of religious life and this, too, was recognized in the new statement.

And, while the older Reformers stressed ethical responsibilities alone, the past century has taught that ethical duties extend to other aspects of Jewish living including keeping a Jewish home, study, prayer, Sabbath and holy days, celebration of the major events in life, and involvement in synagogue. Yet the statement calls upon each Reform Jew to choose and create observances based on individual commitment and knowledge.

Reform takes a strong stand on the state of Israel in its Centenary Perspective, proclaiming:

We are privileged to live in an extraordinary time, one in which a third Jewish commonwealth has been established in our people's ancient homeland. We are bound to that land and to the newly reborn State of Israel by innumerable religious and ethnic ties. We have been enriched by its culture and ennobled by its indomitable spirit. We see it providing unique opportunities for Jewish self-expression. We have both a stake and a responsibility in building the State of Israel, assuring its security and defining its Jewish character. We encourage aliyah *for those who wish to*

First Graduating Class of the Hebrew Union College, 1883

Among the first four rabbis to be ordained at Hebrew Union College was David Phillipson who became a leader of Reform in its second generation and later taught at the College.

find maximum personal fulfillment in the cause of Zion. We demand that Reform Judaism be unconditionally legitimized in the State of Israel.

In some ways the Centenary Perspective retreats somewhat from the older Reform view that Jews must fulfill a mission to the world. It suggests that Jews must be committed to the Jewish people and its future but at the same time be involved in the problems of all humanity.

Clearly, the Reform movement has not stood still. It continues to change and grow in unexpected ways; and its newer developments may yet surprise American Jews. The process of reforming itself seems to be the essence of Reform Judaism today.

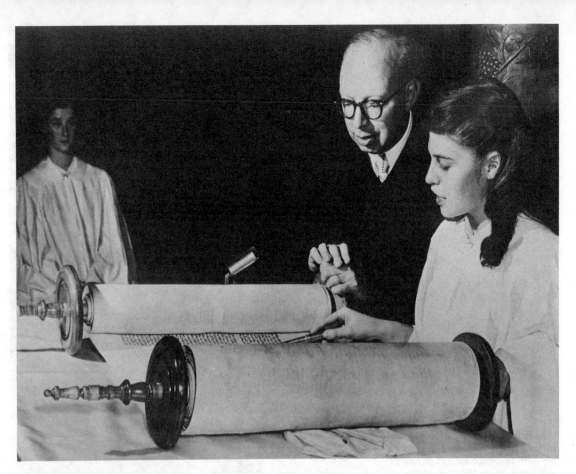

As a movement, the Reform has tried to create new and meaningful traditions such as Bat Mitzvah. At the same time, it has tried to keep those traditions of the past which give Jewish life its special flavor, such as the European tradition of giving flags to children to wave as they march behind the Torah on Simhat Torah.

THE REFORM MOVEMENT IN AMERICA

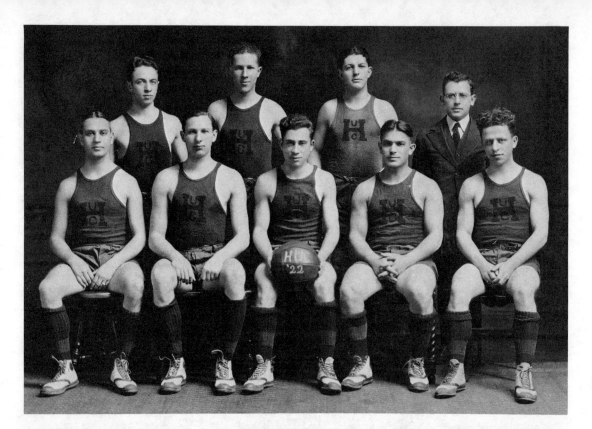

Throughout its history, Reform has tried to combine modern American life with the requirements of Jewish moral law. So, in 1922, the Hebrew Union College had its own basketball team. And in the years of the Viet Nam war, prayers for peace were offered in-house at the Union of American Hebrew Congregations.

THE REFORM
MOVEMENT
IN AMERICA

The Reform movement has also shown a great concern for Jewish education. Today, the movement runs many summer camps which teach Hebrew and Jewish subjects in a relaxed outdoor setting; and the four campuses of the Hebrew Union College-Jewish Institute of Religion train future Reform rabbis, cantors, and educators, as well as scholars and community workers.

The modern concerns of Reform Jews are many and varied. In Los Angeles, at the Hebrew Union College Skirball Museum, students are taken on "walks through Jewish history." Equality for women has also been a Reform priority. Here, the first woman rabbi, Sally Priesand, and Rabbi Edward E. Klein conduct a Simhat Torah service. And at a Holocaust memorial service, women march carrying candles in memory of the six million Jews who were murdered.

Students are taught ethics and Judaism in hundreds of Reform religious schools—and, lately, in several Reform day schools. And in Reform Jewish nursery schools throughout America, children are taught the meaning of Shabbat and the holidays.

**THE REFORM
MOVEMENT
IN AMERICA**

REFORM JUDAISM: BELIEFS AND PRACTICES

Over the years Reform Judaism has changed a great deal. Looking back, it is possible to see two very different kinds of Reform. The first kind existed mainly from the beginnings of the Reform movement until the late 1930s. During this period Reform was very much opposed to traditional ways, which were thought of as "old-fashioned" and "outmoded." This radical kind of Reform has been called "Classical" Reform. And, even though the majority of the movement has changed in recent times, there are still many within the Reform movement who believe in the Classical system.

TWO SYSTEMS OF REFORM

A new kind of Reform was proclaimed in the Columbus Platform of 1937 and is still developing today. It is often called "Modern" Reform, and it has continually adopted more and more traditional practices.

Classical and Modern Reform are very different in their approach to halachah, in their views on Israel and Zionism, and in their ideas about what the Jewish Peoplehood means. Nevertheless, they share many ideas in common. Both groups see Judaism as a changing, evolving, and growing religion; both think of Judaism as the religion of the Jewish people; both teach that the prophetic ideals of social justice and morality are the central ideas of Judaism. Both groups believe that Torah means "teaching" rather than "law," and this means that the halachah or mitzvot are not to be understood as God's Law, but as the creation of human beings—creations which other human beings can change. Reform does not rely on a belief in miracles, mysticism, or a supernatural idea of God. It teaches that Jews have a mission or role to spread monotheism (the belief in one God) to the world and to share the ethical ideals of the Jewish religion with all people.

כתר מלכות • בהונה • תורה כתר • כתר

ציון • תהלה • שיר

Decoration for the top of the Holy Ark. Western Europe, 1773.

GOD

Reform Judaism, unlike Orthodoxy, is very interested in theology or ideas about God. The early Reform rabbis who were strongly influenced by German non-Jewish philosophers such as Kant and Hegel wrote a good deal about God. They described God as a spirit in the universe that maintains order in nature and morality in people. They could not accept the Orthodox view of a supernatural God who performs miracles and interferes with the laws of nature. Miracles such as the parting of the Red Sea or the sun standing still for Joshua were interpreted by Reform scholars as ancient tales or legends that tell more about how people thought of God than how God actually acts in the world.

Modern Reform thinkers have developed new ideas about the meaning of God, and they now speak of a more personal God. Although they do not think of God as a person in the human sense, they believe that God's personality or spirit is present in us and in our world. God is felt in our history, especially in our Jewish history. The Reform scholar Rabbi Eugene B. Borowitz writes that the truest idea of God will inspire us to keep Torah in our lives and preserve the Jewish people. Any idea of God that does not do these two things is improper and false. And to deny the existence of God altogether, he argues, will lead to chaos in our society.

Some Reform thinkers suggest that God is a part of nature and is the living power in the universe. Others believe that God is a force we feel as we struggle to evolve and develop physically and morally. Clearly, Reform ideas about God are rich and diverse. They vary widely from an almost Orthodox, supernatural God who performs miracles and revealed the Torah, to an almost naturalistic idea of God as a power in the universe.

Orthodoxy, as we have seen, firmly believes that God revealed the Torah to Israel at Mount Sinai, that every word of the Torah is sacred and unchangeable, that every law is important. But Reform has a very different view. Reform thinkers believe that only the moral and ethical laws of the Torah are binding forever. Thus, the Ten Commandments and the Golden Rule, "Love your neighbor as yourself," must never be forgotten; but ritual rules such as kashrut and Sabbath restrictions were created by human beings for a specific time in history and are therefore not divine and not necessarily binding on Jews today.

TORAH

Furthermore, Reform thinkers teach that revelation is progressive; that is, God is self-revealing and communicates Divine will and laws to every new generation. In ancient times God revealed rules that were necessary then; in our day God reveals new rules through the people of Israel and their teachers and scholars. These new rules meet the needs of Jews today.

So Reform thinkers do not believe that God gave the entire Torah word for word. They believe that the Bible is a collection of people's thoughts throughout the ages and may even contain primitive ideas and errors. They also teach that the Talmud and the huge body of rabbinic literature are human creations and not eternally valid. On this basic point — God's revelation of Torah and law — Reform differs sharply with Orthodoxy.

Early Reform thinkers were negative toward the mitzvot. Leaders such as Rabbis Isaac Mayer Wise, Kaufmann Kohler, David Einhorn, Samuel Hirsch, and Emil G. Hirsch wrote that ritual commandments were old-fashioned, unnecessary, "oriental," and more useful in middle-Eastern society than in the modern Western world — and thought of many mitzvot as superstition. They complained that the rituals of Orthodoxy set Jews apart from their Christian neighbors and isolated the Jewish people in spiritual ghettos. Wise sneered at kashrut, which he labeled "kitchen Judaism." The more radical, Classical

REFORM IDEAS ABOUT MITZVOT

At first, Confirmation ceremonies, such as the one above held at Temple Emanu-El in New York, replaced the traditional Bar Mitzvah. But soon the Confirmation became an additional ritual, and Bar Mitzvah—and Bat Mitzvah—were reintroduced in almost all Reform synagogues.

Reform rabbis changed Sabbath services to Sunday and introduced late Friday evening services to cope with the problem of failing attendance on Saturday morning. Some attacked circumcision as a barbaric ritual. The ultraradicals argued that the mitzvot were like the outer shell of a nut and should be thrown away to get at the fruit inside. Isaac Mayer Wise, less of a radical than many others, tried to calm them down. In fact, he and several less extreme Reformers actually started a campaign to persuade shopkeepers to close on the Sabbath. But the extreme group remained strong, and more and more of the rituals were dropped. The Pittsburgh Platform of 1885 set the tone of Classical Reform clearly:

> We recognize in the Mosaic legislation a system of training the Jewish people for its mission during its national life in Palestine, and today we accept as binding only the moral laws and maintain only such ceremonies as elevate and sanctify our lives, but reject all such as are not adapted to the views and habits of modern civilization.

The platform added that the laws controlling diet, dress, and priestly purity are not in keeping with modern living and thinking.

The majority of the Reform movement in 1885 readily accepted and adopted the platform and moved swiftly to carry out these principles in synagogue, home, and personal life. Any observances that were thought old-fashioned were discarded. Off went the yarmulke and talit. The organ and mixed choir were introduced and men and women were allowed to sit together. The second day of holiday observances was dropped and some holidays such as Purim and Tisha B'Av were not observed at all. Sabbath laws were eased so that writing, riding, and smoking were allowed. Working on the Sabbath was not considered sinful. Most of the dietary laws were dropped. The ketubah and get were no longer required. Confirmation, usually on Shavuot, replaced Bar Mitzvah at age thirteen. Many of the traditional rules for mourning the dead were eliminated or changed. Mixed marriages of Jews and Christians without conversion were not forbidden.

Sunday school replaced the all-day school or afternoon Hebrew school, and Hebrew was removed from studies in most places. Significantly, Reform gave men and women an equal role in religious life, although it was not until 1972 that the first woman was ordained by the Hebrew Union College.

MORE MODERN POSITIONS

With the arrival of the strongly traditional east European Jews in the 1890s, the Reform movement began to change its attitude in many ways and the old Classical school of Reform was replaced by the Modern school. Many Reform rabbis began to feel that Judaism could not survive merely on high principles or great ideas: It needed concrete actions and symbols, mitzvot and ceremonies, to make it meaningful. Rabbis such as Abba Hillel Silver, Stephen S. Wise, Felix Levy, and Solomon B. Freehof urged that order and control replace disorder and chaos in observance. Finally, the Columbus Platform of 1937 reminded the Reform movement that

> *Judaism as a way of life requires, in addition to its moral and spiritual demands, the preservation of the Sabbath, festivals, and Holy Days, the retention and development of such customs, symbols, and ceremonies as possess inspirational value, the cultivation of distinctive forms of religious art and music, and the use of Hebrew, together with the vernacular, in our worship and instruction.*

Within a short time, the Central Conference of American Rabbis and the Union of American Hebrew Congregations responded to this call. More Hebrew was used in services and religious schools; additional days of classes were added to the Sunday school program; rituals such as *kiddush* (blessing said over wine) on Sabbath eve were reintroduced; and a greater number of Reform Jews began observing kashrut and some of the Sabbath laws. The latest version of the Union prayer book, *Gates of Prayer,* has restored much of the Hebrew of the prayer service, restored some discarded prayers and holiday observances, and even designed a special service for Israel's Independence Day.

A GUIDE FOR REFORM JEWS

Some Reform leaders today are calling for the adoption of an official guide or code to regularize Reform Jewish practices. Rabbi Maurice N. Eisendrath who concentrated for most of his life on issues of social justice and welfare, and who was cool to questions of observance and ritual, suggested once that it was important for Reform

Judaism to end the chaos and confusion by developing guidelines for a Reform Jewish life. Other Reform leaders have actually published guides. Many look forward to a new Reform halachah, based of course on the approval and commitment of the movement's members.

Rabbi Solomon D. Freehof has suggested that the traditional halachah be our guide but not our ruler; that each Jew decide whether or not to observe a particular mitzvah. Eugene Borowitz and Jakob Petuchowski go further to insist that ritual is vital, and mitzvot help a Jew relive the past, insure the survival of the Jewish people, and form a personal tie with God through the *brit* (the covenant) of Sinai.

While Classical Reform was opposed to ritual, today the trend is back to tradition. And the best way to see this change is by looking at the way mixed marriages are viewed. In 1909 the Central Conference of American Rabbis ruled that "mixed marriages are contrary to the tradition of the Jewish religion and should therefore be discouraged." But no action was ever taken against rabbis who performed such marriages (an estimated 40 percent of the Reform rabbis). There was a motion

The Columbus Platform called for "distinctive forms of religious art and music." Jewish artists responded by looking again at old forms and creating new ones such as this modern silver Kiddush cup.

at the 1971 Central Conference condemning rabbis for performing mixed marriages, and, after much debate, it was passed in 1973. Some Reform rabbis formed splinter groups claiming that Reform was becoming too traditional. But the trend is unmistakable. Reform is definitely returning to mitzvot and traditional practices and standards. And it may not be long before there is a guide to how a Reform Jew should live a Jewish life.

THE JEWISH PEOPLE

European Reform was so eager to leave the ghetto and become part of the modern world that it was prepared to give up the independence that the Jewish community had in ghetto times. So the Reformers announced that they were not a separate nation, but that their first loyalty was to the nation in which they lived. American Reform carried this idea even further at the Pittsburgh Conference. There they proclaimed: "We consider ourselves no longer a nation, but a religious community." From that time on Reform Judaism taught that American Jews are American by nationality and that Jews no longer seek to return to the land of Israel because America is their home.

And Reform rejected the idea that Jews are the "Chosen People" of God, substituting instead the "Mission" theory. This theory, introduced in 1885, teaches that Israel's Mission is to teach ethics, morality, and monotheism to all the peoples of the world. Israel must be, as the Prophet Isaiah urged, "a light unto the nations" in order to show them the way to justice, truth, and peace. Isaac Mayer Wise and Kaufmann Kohler firmly believed in the Mission of Israel and predicted that in fifty years Reform Judaism would be the religion of all American Jews.

It was the hope of a simpler time and the Reform rabbis joined Wise and Kohler in their belief. They too taught that it was not a curse to live in exile among the nations of the world, for how else could Reform spread Judaism's message? In their eyes God had blessed Israel by scattering its people throughout the world. The Mission theory was changed slightly in the Columbus Platform of 1937, which referred to the Jewish people as a spiritual nation with a Mission—a responsibility to teach justice, freedom, spirituality, and morality. But even today Reform Jews take the mission role seriously, despite some contemporary thinkers who consider it somewhat prideful.

S ince Reform Jews did not think of Judaism as a nationality, they firmly refused to believe that they must return to their own nation or homeland. They dropped all prayers for return to Zion or for rebuilding Eretz Yisrael or for reestablishing the temple in Jerusalem. Isaac Mayer Wise and Kaufmann Kohler were bitter enemies of the new

Zionist movement. They supported the statement in the Pittsburgh Platform of 1885 that said, "We expect neither a return to Palestine, nor a sacrificial worship under the administration of the sons of Aaron, nor the restoration of any of the laws concerning the Jewish state." For the Reformers, America was the new Zion, the cities or towns in which they lived were the new Jerusalem, and the temples in which they prayed became the temple of ancient Jerusalem.

From 1897 on the Central Conference of American Rabbis and the Union of American Hebrew Congregations were the strongest opponents of the Zionist movement. These organizations argued that Jews would be accused of disloyalty to their country if they sponsored the Zionist cause. Moreover, a return to Zion would defeat Israel's Mission to the rest of the world and would mark a retreat from spiritual greatness to nationalism and politics.

While most Reform Jews agreed with this anti-Zionist position, a few such as Rabbis Stephen S. Wise and Abba Hillel Silver fought to change it. They saw the persecutions of the Jews living in Europe and the changing ideas about nationhood among the peoples of the world, and felt that Zionism was the hope of a Jewish future for many. At last the pro-Zionist position they held took hold in the Reform movement in America, and by the 1930s Reform rabbis were openly urging support for settlers in Palestine. The 1937 Columbus Platform spoke of "the obligation of all Jewry" to aid in upbuilding Palestine as "a Jewish homeland."

Since 1948 the Reform movement has raised millions of dollars for Israel. The movement has built its School of Archaeology in Jerusalem and today all Reform rabbinical students must spend a year of study in Israel. In addition there are more than a dozen Reform congregations in Israel and even a Reform *kibbutz* (collective farm).

Although modern Reform solidly supports the state of Israel and Zionism based on religious values and a belief in God, the movement is opposed to the idea of an Orthodox monopoly in Israel which excludes Reform and treats non-Jews better than it treats liberal Jews. Reform would like to see Israel run according to a progressive interpretation of the Torah with equal rights for all religious groups.

THE JEWISH COMMUNITY

Today the Reform movement has strong ties with Jewry throughout the world. Reform Jews have worked closely with Orthodox, Conservative, Reconstructionist, and secular Jews in raising funds for charity, in defending rights here and abroad, and in helping Soviet Jewry. They are deeply involved in raising money for Israel and supporting Jewish philanthropies. Reform rabbis and laypeople are active in national umbrella groups such as the Synagogue Council of America and the various rabbinical boards.

A keystone of the Reform movement is its commitment to work for social justice and freedom for all people of every religion, race, and nationality. In support of liberal laws and progressive causes, Reform rabbis and laypeople have championed civil rights, fair treatment of laborers, separation of church and state, liberal birth-control laws, and world disarmament. The Pittsburgh Platform's lessons of justice and righteousness as preached by Israel's prophets are a model for social consciousness today. The Columbus Platform stated this clearly when it said that "the love of God is incomplete without the love of fellowman." It called for an end to slavery and tyranny, poverty and prejudice, human suffering and inequality. Reform rabbis have fought for the rights of workers, an end to child labor, and decent wages and working conditions. Many Reform rabbis marched in the South for civil rights for blacks; others have been involved in antiwar campaigns. Through the years Reform has followed an active and liberal course of social action.

INTERFAITH ACTIVITIES

When the Reform movement was founded it welcomed the chance given it by the new, modern freedoms to challenge Christianity. Indeed, some early Reformers called Christianity a pagan religion and charged that it was inferior to Judaism. But this early Reform fervor soon mellowed and a desire for interfaith cooperation began to grow. Both the Pittsburgh and Columbus platforms urged that Judaism and Christianity must fulfill their mission "to aid in the spreading of monotheistic and moral truth" and must cooperate with each other in establishing God's kingdom of justice, truth, and peace on earth.

Some Reform rabbis were carried away by their enthusiasm and even called on Jews to accept Jesus as a prophet and sage of Israel. Others urged Jews to study the Christian Gospels. Today the spirit of interfaith cooperation is strong among Reform rabbis who often exchange pulpits with Christian clergy in order to bring the two faiths closer together and iron out differences and mistrust. A few Reform

17th century menorah in bronze. In looking for new designs, Jewish artists have revived the past and brought to light many such antique treasures.

congregations have actually shared buildings with Protestant churches. The Reform movement has worked hard to break down the walls of hatred and prejudice that have long separated Jews from Christians.

RELIGIOUS PRACTICES

We have studied how Reform ideology denied the authority of halachah and insisted that only the ethical and moral rules are binding on Jews. In their eyes the hundreds of mitzvot that Orthodox Jews practiced were no longer important and they even laughed at times at some of these restrictions. But over the years Reform has loosened its opposition to ritual observances and moved in the direction of tradition. This does not mean that Reform Jews today feel that they *must* observe mitzvot; rather they are more sympathetic, more open to the idea that mitzvot can enrich Jewish life and add to Jewish consciousness.

It is hard to say exactly what the average Reform Jew does in the area of observance because Reform leaves it up to each individual to decide whether or not to follow a particular law. Even though the Reform movement

This ornamental light is a fine example of Jewish artisanship. It is to the credit of the Reform movement that it made us aware of our great heritage of Jewish art and craft.

prefers that people rest on the Sabbath, it does not look upon working as a sin. A Reform Jew has the option to work or not to work. Of course, Reform Jews are expected to attend synagogue on Sabbaths and holidays in order to fulfill their Jewish duty.

Kashrut is usually not observed in Reform homes or synagogues. Riding, smoking, writing, and recreation on the Sabbath are allowed. Reform Jews do not insist on having their children circumcised by a mohel, although most Reform Jews do insist on circumcision. At one time Bar Mitzvah had been replaced by confirmation because the early Reformers argued that it was foolish to consider a thirteen-year-old boy a man. Recently, however, Bar Mitzvah has been restored to most Reform temples and Bat Mitzvah for girls has also been introduced. While marriage to a Jewish mate is certainly the ideal of all Reform families, they do not totally condemn interfaith marriage. Most Reform rabbis do insist that the Christian partner of an interfaith marriage be converted to Judaism, although they do not require traditional rituals of conversion such as circumcision and immersion in a mikveh.

Reform Jews have also revised many of the traditional rituals of death and mourning. Most Reform Jews observe mourning for three days instead of seven, and are not concerned about using only a simple wooden casket for burial.

Reform Jews prefer to call their synagogues "temples" to show that they no longer pray for the rebuilding of the temple in Jerusalem. Men and women sit together in Reform synagogues and instrumental music and choirs are generally a part of the service. The most important service is likely to be the late service on Friday evening when Bar and Bat Mitzvah celebrations are sometimes held. Reform congregations use the *Union Prayer Book* or the new *Gates of Prayer* and conduct most of their prayers in English with some Hebrew prayers and songs. *Kippot* or yarmulkes are not generally required and men do not generally wear a talit or put on tefillin, although lately some Reform temples have begun to allow the yarmulke and talit on an optional basis. The second days of festivals such as Rosh Hashanah, Sukkot, Passover, and Shavuot have been dropped in keeping with the biblical practice. The English sermon is considered the highlight of a Reform worship service and Reform has a liberated attitude toward women, welcoming women as rabbis, cantors, and presidents of their congregations. Most Reform synagogues run a Sunday school, often with one or more additional days of Hebrew school during the week.

In recent years Reform rabbis and leaders have been displeased with the freedom and looseness of Reform Jews to do as they see fit in matters of ritual. As we have seen above, there has been a call for a guide to ritual practices within the movement. Of the guides which have already been published, several call on Reform Jews to enrich their lives by observing such mitzvot as the lighting of Sabbath and festival candles, the saying of kiddush on Friday evening, and the abstention from eating pork in daily meals and leavened products during Passover.

All in all, Reform practice today is closer to the practice of Conservative Jews than ever before, though the Reform Jews still place great emphasis on the laws of justice and righteousness and consider these much more important than the laws of ritual observance. Perhaps this is fitting, since it was the Reform movement which in many ways gave rise to Conservative Judaism.

CONSERVATIVE JUDAISM

TRADITION AND CHANGE

Conservative Judaism, like Reform, had its beginnings in Germany. Many thought that Reform had gone too far in discarding and changing traditional practices. They sought a middle ground and organized a counter-Reform movement. The leader of this new Conservative group was the famous rabbi and talmudic scholar Zachariah Frankel of Prague.

Frankel was deeply hurt when the Frankfort Rabbinical Conference of 1845 ruled that the use of the Hebrew language was no longer required in the synagogue. He believed otherwise. Along with a group of moderate reformers, he founded the Jewish Theological Seminary of Breslau in 1854 and began to teach a new version of Judaism. The group was soon given the strange name of the "Positive-Historical" school of Judaism. They were "positive" because they wanted to preserve the mitzvot and halachah, unlike the Reform movement. And they were "historical" because they believed that Judaism and its laws and institutions had grown and changed through the centuries, and that it was vital to study that historical growth so as to understand Judaism properly. The Positive-Historical group did not enjoy wide success in Europe. Like the Reform movement, the great victories of Conservative Judaism would be won in the New World.

THE SHIFT TO AMERICA

The early builders of the Conservative movement in America were rabbis and laypeople who were neither Orthodox nor Reform. They might best be called "traditional" Jews. While they disliked the extremes to which the Reform group was heading, they realized the need to change and update the Jewish laws and practices. In America the first important leader was Reverend Isaac Leeser (1806–68), who served as rabbi of Philadelphia's Mikveh Israel Synagogue. Leeser preached his sermons in English, translated the Bible into English, wrote school texts, edited a magazine called *The Occident,* helped raise funds to support colonies in Palestine, and founded the first rabbinical school, Maimonides College of Philadelphia. He disliked being called "Orthodox" and rejected the term "Reform." Today we can see that he was the forerunner of the modern Conservative rabbi.

Leeser's work was continued by Rabbis Benjamin Szold of Baltimore, Sabato Morais of Philadelphia, and Alexander Kohut, Marcus Jastrow, and other rabbis in New York. The new movement also attracted a number of

Isaac Leeser (1806-1868), rabbi, author, editor, and staunch champion of traditional Judaism. He was not Orthodox and did not like being called Reform.

important laypeople including Joseph Blumenthal, Henrietta Szold, and Cyrus Adler. Some of these early leaders of Conservatism were still close to Orthodoxy; some even joined the Orthodox movement in the end. Others were close to Reform but objected to the radicalism and extremism of Wise, Kohler, and Einhorn. However, they were united in their determination to hold to tradition while somehow modernizing traditional practices.

At first some of these traditionalists tried to work within the Reform group. In fact, Reverend Sabato Morais actually helped Isaac Mayer Wise to set up the Hebrew Union College. But Morais and his friends were disturbed as Reform temples introduced worship services on Sundays, and furious when nonkosher food was served at the graduation banquet of the first class at Hebrew Union College in 1883. The publication of the Pittsburgh Platform of 1885 was the last straw. It became clear to Morais and his co-workers that they would have to build a new rabbinical school, one that would save traditional Judaism.

THE JEWISH THEOLOGICAL SEMINARY

In 1886 Sabato Morais gathered a group of supporters at New York's Shearith Israel synagogue, the Spanish and Portuguese congregation, to create a new seminary for the training of traditional rabbis. Some suggested that the school be called the Orthodox Seminary, but the majority wanted a more neutral name. They finally agreed on "The Jewish Theological Seminary of America."

Rabbi Alexander Kohut was already using the term "Conservative" in his writings and speeches. For him, "Conservative" meant two things: First, the movement would seek to "conserve" or "preserve" Jewish tradition; and second, it would be "conservative" in opposing the drastic changes of Reform while accepting the necessary changes of a less revolutionary type. The name stuck. The new school made its purpose clear in its charter, which stated that it would be "faithful to Mosaic Law and ancestral tradition," and it would teach the Bible and rabbinic literature faithfully, training its rabbis in Jewish knowledge, Hebrew language, and Jewish law.

With Sabato Morais as its first president, the Jewish Theological Seminary opened in 1887 with an enrollment of eight students. The faculty was only part-time and Morais himself traveled from his home in Philadelphia to teach at the school in New York. Students were required to earn a degree at some other college in addition to their rabbinic diploma. The first rabbi was ordained at the seminary in 1893.

As with the other new seminaries, the Jewish Theological Seminary had monetary problems from the start. When Morais died in 1897 he left no successor and the school was struggling and losing support. By 1901 it seemed that the seminary would have to close for lack of money, students, and teachers. But a group of dedicated laypeople came to the rescue. Dr. Cyrus Adler and the Jewish philanthropist Jacob Schiff were determined to save the school. Schiff and several of his Reform friends were convinced that the poor, east European immigrants would never feel comfortable in the German Reform temples with their English prayers and organ music. It seemed to them that American Jewish life required an alternative kind of synagogue worship and a different kind of rabbi. So Adler and Schiff raised a large amount of money to save the seminary. They asked Dr. Solomon Schechter of Cambridge, England, to come to America to head the school.

Schechter was born in Rumania in 1849 and was educated in Vienna and Berlin. He taught Hebrew and Talmud at Cambridge and the University of London and gained a world-wide reputation when he discovered the Cairo *genizah*. The genizah was a huge treasure of Hebrew manuscripts that had been buried in an ancient synagogue. Schechter devoted many years to the study of these manuscripts and his careful approach and artful study became known far and wide. Schiff and Adler could hardly have made a better choice.

During his presidency of the Jewish Theological Seminary of America, Schechter stamped his personality on the school and the young Conservative movement. He built a fine faculty of scholars and teachers, watched over and directed the establishment of the library for the school, and started a Hebrew Teacher's Institute. He insisted on scholarship based on historical studies and criticism, and made it the policy of the seminary that all views could be expressed freely. The seminary stood for "the preservation in America of the knowledge and practice of historical Judaism, as contained in the Laws of Moses and expounded by the Prophets and Sages of Israel in biblical and Talmudic writings." Schechter's leadership was not only felt within the school; it set the tone for Conservative Judaism and helped shape the entire movement.

Upon Schechter's death in 1915, the presidency of the seminary fell to Dr. Cyrus Adler who directed it until 1940 when he died. The next president was Dr. Louis Finkelstein, an American-born graduate of the seminary who guided its continued growth and success. During his long term of office, both the seminary and the Conservative movement grew. A branch

Sabato Morais (1823-1897), rabbi of the Sephardi Mikveh Israel Congregation in Philadelphia and founder of The Jewish Theological Seminary of America.

Solomon Schechter (1850-1915), scholar, spokesman, and philosopher of Conservative Judaism.

called The University of Judaism was opened in Los Angeles, The Jewish Museum was established in New York, and a school in Jerusalem was founded. In 1972 Rabbi Finkelstein retired and Rabbi Gerson Cohen became the new president.

Today there are about one thousand students and one hundred faculty members at the various branches of the seminary.

THE RABBIS ORGANIZE

In 1901 a rabbinical organization was founded to support the Conservative movement, but it was not until 1919 that it took as its official name The Rabbinical Assembly of America. The assembly was set up to promote Conservative Judaism, to aid the Jewish Theological Seminary, to help its members, the Conservative rabbis, by protecting their rights and securing their pensions for retirement, and to assist Jewish scholars. Today the organization is called simply the Rabbinical Assembly and it has a thousand members in several countries.

THE CONSERVATIVE MOVEMENT

As the number of rabbis grew and the number of synagogues practicing Conservative Judaism became greater, the need for a synagogue group was felt. So the United Synagogue of America was set up in 1913 under the leadership of Dr. Schechter, Cyrus Adler, Rabbi Mordecai M. Kaplan, and several other seminary graduates. At first there were twenty-two congregations. Meeting in New York they defined their purposes as:

The advancement of the cause of Judaism in America and the maintenance of Jewish tradition in its historic continuity.

To assert and establish loyalty to the Torah and its historic exposition.

To further the observance of the Sabbath and the dietary laws.

To preserve in the service the reference to Israel's past and the hopes for Israel's restoration.

To maintain the traditional character of the liturgy with Hebrew as the language of prayer.

To foster Jewish religious life in the home, as expressed in traditional observances.

To encourage the establishment of Jewish religious schools. . . .

Any congregation that worshipped without head coverings or used the Reform *Union Prayer Book* was barred from joining the new group, although congregations that allowed men and women to sit together during worship or used an organ could belong.

Solomon Schechter was chosen as the first president of the United Synagogue, and he immediately called for more decorum at services, the use of English sermons, higher religious school standards for boys and girls, and more religious observances in the home.

The United Synagogue grew slowly. It added the National Women's League in 1917, the Young People's League in 1921, and the National Federation of Jewish Men's Clubs in 1929. In 1951 it established the United Synagogue Youth. Today the United Synagogue helps sponsor Ramah Camps throughout the country, the Leaders Training Fellowship, a college organization called Atid, and the Solomon Schechter Day Schools. But it was in the years just after World War II that the Conservative movement really gained importance as Jews flocked to the suburbs of the large cities and started new Conservative congregations.

Today there are about 830 Conservative synagogues in North America with approximately one and a half million members. When Jews in Argentina, Israel, India, Central and South America, and other countries began to found Conservative synagogues, a new need developed for a worldwide organization. In 1959 the World Council of Synagogues was established to aid the growth of the Conservative movement throughout the world.

The Conservative movement has always viewed Israel as special. In 1926 the United Synagogue helped found the Yeshurun Synagogue in Jerusalem. In 1962 the seminary built its student center in Neve Schechter in Jerusalem and later took over the Schocken Institute for Jewish Research. Today all Conservative rabbinical students must spend one year of study in Israel. There are more than twenty Conservative synagogues and about eighty

Conservative rabbis living and working there. The World Council of Synagogues set up its headquarters in Jerusalem in 1972.

THE GROWTH OF THE MOVEMENT

What caused the Conservative movement to grow so rapidly after World War II ? As you have just read, one major reason was the movement of the Jews away from the centers of the cities into the suburbs. In these new suburbs there were no Orthodox congregations, and many Jews found the Reform temples too extreme. Most of the new suburbanites were Jews who were used to east European-style shuls in their old neighborhoods and who liked the traditional practices as they had learned them. Still they wanted changes, the kind of changes the Conservative movement wanted. So they established Conservative synagogues and hired graduates of the Jewish Theological Seminary as their rabbis.

America was a good ground for Conservatism to grow. This moderate, middle-of-the-road philosophy was practical and fit the mood of the United States, a country that had always avoided extremes in politics, economics, and religion. It was natural that America's Jews felt more at home and comfortable as part of a moderate, nonrevolutionary movement that balanced Orthodoxy and Reform by combining the traditions of one with the liberalism of the other.

And, although the Conservative movement is not growing as rapidly today as it did in the past, it can look back to many accomplishments and ahead to many new challenges. Can the movement finally create a body of laypeople who will live up to the principles set by its leaders, rabbis, and teachers? Will the Conservative movement eventually join with the Reform? Will it succeed in changing halachah while preserving tradition? These are questions only time can answer. But there is no doubt that the Conservative movement has been the fastest-growing and most dynamic Jewish religious movement in America in the twentieth century.

In the synagogue and in the home, Conservative Jews try to preserve traditions, such as the wearing of tallit at morning prayers and the lighting of the Hanukkah menorah, while changing halachah to meet the needs of modern times.

Central to the Conservative movement has been the Seminary founded in 1886 which held its first classes at Congregation Shearith Israel in New York City (shown opposite). Rabbis, students, and scholars meet at The Jewish Theological Seminary, sharing concerns and ideas, praying together daily, and celebrating such holidays as Sukkot in the traditional manner.

Study and observance form the Conservative way of life;
Torah is at its center. Unlike the Reform movement, which
leaves decisions of law basically up to the individual; and
unlike the Orthodox, who change the law hardly at all
and then over a considerable period of time; the
Conservative movement has tried to deal with issues of
Jewish law in a careful, but realistic way. One of the
largest issues facing the Conservative movement today is
the question of equal Jewish rights for women. After much
debate and discussion, a woman was recently called to the
reading of the Torah at an official United Synagogue
Convention. But the question remains unsolved.

THE CONSERVATIVE
MOVEMENT
IN AMERICA

For the Conservative Jew, changes in the halachah must come only as the
result of careful study. Much of that study goes on here, in the reading room
of the excellent Jewish Theological Seminary library.

Jewish learning never ends, whether it takes place in the fine Ramah camps, in the Solomon Schechter Day Schools, in synagogue religious schools, in adult study groups, or in the several branches of the Seminary. To change the future, the Conservative Jew must know the past.

CONSERVATIVE JUDAISM: BELIEFS AND PRACTICES

It is difficult to describe the basic beliefs of Conservative Judaism. First, Conservative Judaism is a movement made up of several groups with several different philosophies and beliefs. In fact, the Conservative movement includes people who are very nearly Orthodox, people who are almost Reform, and those in the middle. Also, unlike the Reform movement which has issued platforms stating basic beliefs from time to time, the Conservative movement has not issued many formal statements or platforms. The Conservative group has preferred to be practical and allow living situations to set the course without interference from formal creeds.

Yet some Conservative leaders would like to see a formal platform or creed because they claim that no one really knows what Conservative Judaism should mean, and that too much leeway is allowed the members and congregations within the United Synagogue. A few have actually tried to write down such a basic set of beliefs, but it has been difficult for them to win any agreement. Despite this, Conservative Jews do seem to share several basic ideas.

Conservative Judaism believes that tradition is vital and must be preserved. At the same time, it sees Judaism as more than just halachah or religion or creed, but rather as a religious civilization or culture that has changed and developed through history. It is important, therefore, to study the historical growth of Jewish laws, customs, ideas, and institutions in order to understand them fully. Conservatives further think that this ongoing process of change in Judaism can be brought about by evolutionary rather than revolutionary means, that is, slowly instead of all-at-once. So the two keys to understanding the Conservative movement are the ideas of *tradition* and *change*.

GOD

Conservative Judaism is like Reform in that its thinkers and leaders have taught varied views about God. Some believe in a personal, supernatural God who listens to prayers and is keenly aware of human events. Thus, Solomon Schechter wrote that God is not a mere idea but a spirit found everywhere—in the temple, in the court of law, in the family, on the farm, in the marketplace, and at moments when we enforce God's laws. Rabbi Ben Zion Bokser wrote that God is not a person, but is greater than any person; God's personality or presence fills the world.

The late religious thinker Professor Abraham J. Heschel wrote several books on the subject. Heschel was a mystic. He believed that we should not try to prove the existence of God but we should feel God's spirit or presence in the order of the universe and in the moral laws we find among human beings. According to Heschel's belief, we feel a basic "amazement" when we experience the glories of nature and history, an amazement that we cannot express properly or put into words. We also feel God's presence when we pray, study Torah, and perform mitzvot.

On the other end, there are many Conservative thinkers who do not accept the idea of a supernatural or personal God. Rabbi Mordecai M. Kaplan, for example, wrote of God as a power or process in people and in the universe that makes for human salvation or fulfillment. Rabbi Robert Gordis believes that God is the creative power in the universe and the force behind social, political, and scientific progress in the world. Gordis says that God may be found both in the order of nature and in the course of our history. We cannot know what God *is*; we can only feel God's workings through our world and the people in it.

TORAH

Orthodoxy builds its faith on the absolute belief that God gave every word of the Torah at Mount Sinai, and Reform believes that only the ethical rules were revealed there. Conservative Judaism tries to steer a course between the two. Nearly all Conservative thinkers accept the idea that God revealed the Torah to

Israel. But there are some who believe that the revealing of Torah, or *revelation*, happened only once in history, while others consider revelation to be an on-going process by which each generation of Jews uncovers more and more of God's word.

But what does "revelation" mean? Most Conservative thinkers do not believe that God actually spoke each word of Torah to Moses and Israel. Indeed, biblical studies have shown that there are different sources in the Bible text, and that Moses could not have been the only writer. So the majority of Conservative thinkers do not believe that the *entire* Bible is the word of God. But they do believe that the basic core of Torah, the important parts, is Divine. Without this notion the faith would crumble.

The reason that Conservative Jews cannot accept the Orthodox position that the Torah is the complete and final word of God is because change and growth would then be impossible. Nor can they agree with the Reform movement that only ethical rules are God-given, since it may very well be that God is concerned with the observance of ritual laws as well as ethical laws.

Furthermore, Conservative thinkers, unlike Orthodox thinkers, believe that revelation is a two-way process, or a dialogue between God and humanity. The core of God's truth cannot be denied, but the ways in which we think about that truth as developed in the Bible and Talmud are our own and therefore may contain human errors and are subject to change. Conservative Jews believe, then, that the Bible and Jewish laws are our response to God's call; the mitzvah is human interpretation and application of Divine principles.

HALACHAH

So the Conservative movement does accept halachah and does have a positive attitude to Jewish law. But interpretation and reinterpretation of the law is left to us. While Conservative Jews accept such basic and fundamental laws as Sabbath observance, holy day observance and kashrut, Jewish marriage and divorce, the need for a good Jewish education and the study of the Hebrew language, and the ethical rules of the faith, they also realize the need to update some Jewish laws. For example, Conservative Judaism says that it is so important for a Jew to attend

Even in building synagogues, such as Kneses Tifereth Israel of Port Chester, New York, Conservative Jews show a concern for making Judaism a vibrant reality for today.

synagogue that driving to synagogue is permitted if a Jew lives too far away to walk. The Conservative movement allows a person to eat dairy meals even in a nonkosher restaurant. And Conservative rabbis have made some important changes in laws concerning marriage and divorce. For example, they have solved the problem of a woman whose husband cannot or is not willing to give her a divorce by allowing a *bet din* (Jewish court) to annul or dissolve the marriage. These are but a few of the sweeping changes made by the Rabbinical Assembly's Law Committee since it was reorganized in 1948.

Still, the question of who has the right to change laws and on what basis is a difficult one. Solomon Schechter agreed that law is basic to Judaism because a movement cannot survive on high-minded ideas alone. But he believed that the living body of people—including prophets, psalmists, sages, and rabbis—through the ages would have the final word in changing Jewish laws, accepting some, doing away with others.

The great talmudic scholar Professor Louis Ginzberg taught that we must study the historical development of each law. He pointed out that Jewish law was never dead or frozen; it grew and changed and kept up with new social and economic conditions. Ginzberg wrote that "law is religion and religion is law," and that Jewish law is vital to Judaism and the Jewish people. But Ginzberg wanted to be sure that the modernization of the law would not be left in the hands of the average person or the unlearned. His position on Jewish law had a great impact on the leading scholars of Conservatism, people such as Louis Finkelstein and Boaz Cohen. Robert Gordis, whose thoughts about God we have just read, was also a follower of Ginzberg's views. In Gordis' words, "Growth is the law of life, and law is the life of Judaism." Gordis believes in revelation as a continuing process and so he suggests that the living Torah builds on Moses' creation just as an oak tree grows from an acorn. In this way, he says, the rules that were made before our time allow us to make rules for our own time. Gordis believes that halachah is necessary for four reasons: 1) it ties us to the universe in which we live, 2) it teaches us ethical and social values, 3) it adds beauty to our lives, and 4) it binds each Jew to the Jewish people and the community.

In general then we see that the Conservative movement is committed to halachah and mitzvot. Some Conservative thinkers believe that we must be more bold in changing certain rules; others criticize the Conservative movement for moving too quickly. But all firmly believe that Jewish law must be modernized and updated in order to keep it alive. And within the Conservative movement it is the task of the Law Committee of the Rabbinical Assembly to work out these changes.

THE JEWISH PEOPLE

The Conservative movement places great stress on the concept of Jewish peoplehood. It believes that Torah, mitzvot, and Jewish values are designed to keep the Jewish people alive and it welcomes any means of strengthening Jewish creative survival. Orthodoxy's main concern is halachah; Reform stresses God and ethics; but Conservatism builds its main structure around the Jewish people.

Many Conservative thinkers—from Solomon Schechter to Mordecai M. Kaplan, from Dr. Cyrus Adler to Rabbi Louis Finkelstein—have preached the importance of *klal yisrael,* the world Jewish community and our responsibility to help one another as Jews. So the Conservative movement has looked out for Jews here in America and in countries all over the world and has been eager to cooperate with all Jews whatever their religious beliefs.

The Conservative movement also accepts the idea of the chosen people. Conservative Jews believe that Israel was chosen by God for a special purpose or reason: to spread the teachings of Torah to the nations of the world. But being chosen is not so much a privilege as a duty, for Jews are expected to live up to a higher standard of ethics and behavior. In the words of Abraham Joshua Heschel, "Israel is a holy people whose task is to prove that in order to be a people we have to be more than a people."

Imposing and stately, the building of the Conservative Congregation Beth El of Rochester, New York, reminds us that the Jews have built a solid community in America. From this base, the movement has felt secure in reaching out a helping hand to Eretz Yisrael.

THE LAND OF ISRAEL

The Conservative movement has always been in favor of the reestablishment of the state of Israel. Isaac Leeser worked to raise money for farm colonies in Israel, and Conservative rabbis and laypeople were among the early founders of the Zionist movement in America. Rabbi Marcys Jastrow, for one, was vice-president of the Federation of American Zionists, and Henrietta Szold founded Hadassah, the women's Zionist organization. Solomon Schechter was another ardent Zionist, though he fought against any Zionism that would merely be secular and political. He believed that Zionism must not only rebuild a Jewish homeland but also revive the Jewish religion and its spiritual values. He envisioned Israel as a spiritual center for world Jewry. Schechter was active in the Zionist Organization of America and was a delegate at several Zionist congresses and conventions.

Schechter's followers and students carried on his passion for Zion and the religious ideal of Israel reborn. As early as 1928 the Rabbinical Assembly at its annual conventions publicly called for support of colonists in Palestine and aid to the Zionist movement. Conservative rabbis and laypeople have loyally supported the United Jewish Appeal to help settle Jews in Israel and have fought for continued support for the new nation of Israel ever since it came into being in 1948. Many Conservative thinkers have urged that Jews should go on aliyah (settle in Israel permanently). Of course they do not suggest, as some Zionists do, that Jewish life is impossible outside of Israel. But they do say that a full, spiritual life can only be realized in Eretz Yisrael. This is undoubtedly why so many Conservative rabbis, educators, and laypeople have gone to settle in Israel.

In the past years two important issues concerning Israel have affected the Conservative movement. One is the question of allowing Conservative rabbis to practice as official rabbis in the state of Israel. The problem is that the Orthodox movement has gained control over the religious life of the new state and so Reform and Conservative rabbis have been kept from such basic things as performing weddings and conversions. It will probably be some time before this problem is settled, and it is a problem that both the Conservative and Reform rabbis are cooperating to resolve.

The second problem concerns the World Zionist Organization. Clearly the Conservative movement has always been Zionistic, yet the World Zionist Organization has never allowed Conservatives to be a part of its conferences or to vote on any Zionist issues. Now, however, it seems likely that the Conservative movement will soon become a full-fledged voting member of the World Zionist Organization.

THE JEWISH COMMUNITY

It has always been important as far as the Conservative movement is concerned to cooperate with Jews of all opinions. Solomon Schechter had stressed the value of klal yisrael and had tried earnestly to cooperate with the Reform leaders of his time although he disagreed with their philosophy. Ever since, it has been a tradition of the Conservative movement to work with the other Jewish movements and groups.

Over the years the Conservative movement has fought for a stronger, more unified Jewish community. Conservative leaders have campaigned to aid Israel and Soviet Jewry, and to look after the educational and financial needs of all Jews at home and abroad. Rabbi Mordecai M. Kaplan taught his students at the Jewish Theological Seminary of the need to build a strong Jewish community; and his students learned this lesson well.

On the other hand, the Conservative movement has not been as deeply involved with social action as has the Reform group. Yet there were those Conservative leaders who were. In fact, the early Conservative rabbis such as Jastrow, Szold, and Morais actually preached from their pulpits about the need to treat the striking clothing workers more fairly, and they urged their congregants to assist the new immigrants in their adjustment to American life. In 1934 a full statement on social justice was issued by the Rabbinical Assembly reminding its members that the most important teaching of Jewish tradition is the message of social justice.

A number of Conservative rabbis marched with blacks in the South to support their cause. And other causes of social justice were supported too: nuclear disarmament, atomic test ban treaties, liberal immigration laws, and the right to abortion. The Conservative movement has always fought for a separation of church and state and has traditionally opposed federal aid to Jewish day schools and other parochial schools. (Recently, as the Solomon Schechter Day Schools have found it more and more difficult to meet their huge budgets, many Conservative laypeople and rabbis have changed their minds and have suggested that government should give aid to private schools. So on this issue, the movement is now somewhat divided.)

INTERFAITH ACTIVITIES

Conservative Jews have been just as willing to be a part of interfaith activities as inter-Jewish ones. The movement believes that it is important for various religious groups to join together in order to understand each other and cooperate in building a better world. Thus, Rabbi Finkelstein worked hard to bring together Christian, Moslem, and Oriental religious leaders at the seminary in the hope of breaking down prejudices and encouraging friendships. Robert Gordis called for religious dialogue and discussions, but only if the Christians would agree to respect the Hebrew Bible, cease blaming Jews for the death of Jesus, and stop seeking to convert Jews to Christianity. Rabbi Abraham Joshua Heschel worked closely with Cardinal Bea in helping the Vatican shape new attitudes toward the Jewish people.

Here too the Conservative leaders differ in their ideas and approaches. Some insist that frank and open discussions by philosophers and scholars are necessary to end prejudice once and for all. Others believe that such discussions are a waste of time. Generally, though, most Conservative thinkers believe that we must have open discussions with Christian leaders and philosophers so that they may understand what we believe about God, Torah, and Israel, and why Judaism still has a role to play in today's world. And most agree, too, that such discussions should be conducted only by qualified scholars, rabbis, and theologians.

RELIGIOUS PRACTICES

Officially, Conservative Judaism expects its members to abide by the mitzvot and to lead a life based on halachah. In reality, few Conservative laypeople live up to that ideal, and the gap between theory and practice in the Conservative movement is the greatest of any Judaic group. Nevertheless, the program of Conservatism clearly indicates that it believes in a growing, dynamic system of Jewish law by which Jews must live if Judaism is to flourish.

A Conservative Jew is expected to refrain from working, riding, writing, or smoking on the Sabbath. (However, a Jew may ride to and from the synagogue on the Sabbath and festivals if the distance is too great for walking.) Conservative Jews are permitted to use electricity on Shabbat and the festivals since the Law Committee of the Rabbinical Assembly has ruled that electricity is not the same as fire, which is prohibited. The committee also recommended that the observance of the second day of festivals (Passover, Shavuot, Sukkot) shall be optional so that our calendar will be the same as that used in Israel. But only a few synagogues have dropped the second day.

There are other areas in which Conservative Judaism is more flexible about halachah. A Conservative Jew is expected to observe kashrut, but may eat dairy in a nonkosher restaurant. A Conservative Jew must marry only a Jewish mate; and no Conservative rabbi will officiate at an intermarriage unless the non-Jewish partner converts first. But the Conservative movement has been more willing than the Orthodox to accept such converts. When a marriage ends in divorce, a Conservative Jew must receive a Jewish get, or divorce, before remarrying.

Male children are to be circumcised ritually and given Hebrew names; female children are named in the synagogue. Conservative Jews are expected to receive a Jewish education, and today more children than ever are receiving intensive Jewish educations at Solomon Schechter Day Schools. In fact, by 1978, there were more than ninety-five hundred children in these schools. Bar Mitzvah and Bat Mitzvah ceremonies are marked by almost all Conservative boys and girls, and many young people continue their studies in high schools run by synagogues and communities. Death and mourning rules are fairly traditional, although most Conservative Jews will tear a ribbon rather than their garment as a sign of mourning, and few Conservative rabbis insist that the dead person be dressed in a shroud. The mourning period is the traditional seven days, and a Conservative Jew is expected to recite kaddish daily for a loved one.

Most Conservative Jewish males do not wear skull caps all the time; rather, they wear them at prayer or when studying the Torah. Similarly, Conservative women do not cover their hair with wigs or scarves. Conservative males are expected to pray daily and to wear a talit and tefillin and recite the various prayers before and after meals. A Conservative woman is required to run a kosher home and light candles for Sabbath and the holy days. But she does not usually go to the mikveh, except for conversion.

The worship service and the pattern of prayer in Conservative synagogues differ from congregation to congregation. For example, some synagogues permit the use of an organ and have choirs of men and women, while others do not. Most conduct services on the second day of *Yom Tov*, but a few do not. All include some English prayers in the service and have an English sermon or Torah discussion, although the length of the Torah reading may vary. Almost all Conservative synagogues allow men and women to sit together during prayer services. In many congregations the main service is the late one on Friday evening. There is usually more reading in English at this service than at Sabbath morning services.

As in the Reform movement, there has been some dissatisfaction with traditional prayers, and the Rabbinical Assembly has been striving to publish new prayer books in a more modern style that includes material by modern poets. In fact, a new high holiday *Mahzor* has recently been issued and a new Sabbath *Siddur* and Passover *Haggadah* should soon follow.

Almost all Conservative synagogues are synagogue centers that contain Hebrew schools, Hebrew high schools, youth groups, adult classes, and many other activities.

Recently, Conservative synagogue services have been affected by the women's rights issue. The Rabbinical Assembly's Law Committee has taken steps to equalize the role of women in congregational life. The committee suggested that women be given the right to be called to the Torah and be counted in the *minyan* (the ten Jews needed for congregational worship). And the Rabbinical Assembly and the Jewish Theological Seminary are now considering the possibility of allowing women to study in order to become rabbis. At present about one-third of the Conservative synagogues have given girls and women equal rights at services. Many others allow women to hold office in the congregation. So while it appears that the issue of women's rights will be debated for some time, the current trend is toward granting females equal rights with males in every way.

Conservative Jews are expected to lead ethical and moral lives, to give charity, to help needy friends and neighbors, and to act in an honest, kind, moral, and decent way toward all. For Conservative Jews, the ethical laws and rules of Judaism are even more important than the ritual laws because, in the Conservative view, the purpose of Judaism is to shape us into better and more honorable human beings. Theoretically then, Conservative Jews are expected to live according to the demands of Jewish law and Torah in every way.

The symbols of Judaism—past and present—are part of the life of the Conservative Jew. Tradition speaks of "the crown of Torah," and Western Jews have often placed a real crown on the sefer Torah to show its importance.

RECON-STRUCTIONIST JUDAISM

FROM PHILOSOPHY TO MOVEMENT

The youngest of the religious movements in American Judaism is the Reconstructionist movement. It is particularly an American movement, unlike the other religious groups that began in Europe and were transplanted to America. Born in 1922, its leaders and thinkers are all American and most of its ideas are rooted in American philosophy and thought.

Of course Reconstructionism did borrow some of its important theories from European philosophers and social scientists. For example, Reconstructionism borrowed from the Russian-Jewish historian Simon Dubnow the theory that Jewish communities must live as independent, creative units in every country in the world, each developing its own culture and civilization. Reconstructionism was also influenced by the Russian-Jewish philosopher Ahad Ha-am who wrote that Israel should become the cultural and spiritual center of Jewry and tie the Jewish communities of the world together. And Reconstructionism took over ideas from French and British thinkers as well. It adopted some of its ideas about God from the English philosophers. And it accepted the view of the French sociologist Emile Durkheim that rituals help keep a people together and religion is basically a social or group experience.

But even though these ideas came from European sources, the Reconstructionist movement is American in a unique way. It is based on the work of one great man who created, built, taught, and spread its philosophy throughout America. That man is Rabbi Mordecai M. Kaplan. Dr. Kaplan (whom we have studied before because he taught at the Jewish Theological Seminary and was a part of the Conservative movement for many years) devoted more than seventy years of his life to "the advancement of Judaism as a religious civilization, to the upbuilding of *Eretz Yisrael*, and to the furtherance of universal freedom, justice and peace." In a way, the biography of Mordecai Kaplan is the history of the Reconstructionist movement.

Kaplan was born in 1881 near Vilna, Poland. His father was an Orthodox rabbi and his mother was a learned and pious woman. From the start, his parents wished him to become a rabbi. In 1889 Mordecai's father left Poland to take a job in New York as the assistant to Rabbi Jacob Joseph, the newly chosen chief rabbi of New York City. A year later Mordecai and his mother and sister followed.

On the way to America Mordecai had two experiences that showed him how hard it is to live as an Orthodox Jew in a world that is largely non-Jewish. The first occurred in Paris where the family lived for a year. There he attended school and was forced to go to classes on Saturday. He had to decide whether or not to write his lessons on Shabbat. For an Orthodox Jewish child, it was a painful problem.

And it was a problem he had to face soon again. On the ship to America there was a fireworks display

The official emblem of the Reconstructionist movement is like a chart showing how we in the Diaspora are linked to Zion (Israel) by our religion, ethics, and culture.

planned for French Independence Day. But it was planned for the Sabbath, and his mother did not want him to watch the fireworks. He was disappointed and unhappy. And he never forgot how he felt that day. Later in writing about what it means to live in two worlds—a Jewish world and a non-Jewish one—at once, Kaplan recalled these two experiences and spoke about them at length.

In the meantime, Mordecai's father made sure that his child received a good private education in Torah as well as a public school education. Mordecai was a brilliant student. He studied hard for school and listened well to the many famous visitors who passed through the Kaplan home. One, the famous Bible scholar and critic Arnold B. Ehrlich, read his new Bible commentary to Mordecai and it stirred up doubts in Mordecai's mind as to whether Moses really wrote the Torah as he had been taught. Later Kaplan became interested in Jewish philosophy and began to study works such as Maimonides' *Guide to the Perplexed*. Always he questioned.

Kaplan studied at the Jewish Theological Seminary of America and at New York's City College and Columbia University. He was ordained a rabbi in 1902. His first position was as associate rabbi in a prominent Orthodox synagogue in New York. In 1908, on his honeymoon in Europe, he received semichah (ordination) again—this time from a famous Orthodox rabbi.

But his path led him away from Orthodoxy. He had become closely associated with Solomon Schechter, and in 1909 he left the Orthodox pulpit to become dean of the new Teachers Institute of the Jewish Theological Seminary. Here Kaplan trained hundreds of Hebrew teachers and, after he was appointed to the seminary's Rabbinical School faculty, also helped train and influence three generations of rabbis. All the time he continued his studies of Jewish thought and philosophy, psychology, and sociology, and continued to ponder about God, Torah, mitzvot, and Jewish peoplehood. Though he continued to observe the mitzvot in the fashion of an Orthodox Jew, his ideas were becoming less and less Orthodox.

Kaplan was always a man of action, a hard worker in community projects. In 1908 he helped found the Kehillah of New York. The Kehillah was an attempt to unify all the Jewish organizations of New York City into one group. For many years he tried to strengthen Jewish education through one of the branches of the Kehillah, the Board of Jewish Education.

He was also an active Zionist. And—though it seems strange—he was one of the founders of the Orthodox Young Israel movement in 1912 and tried to inspire young Jews to return to the synagogues. Of course, as he continued to question Orthodox beliefs about God, revelation, and the authorship of the Torah, he and the Young Israel movement went their separate ways. Still he continued to think of himself as Orthodox. In 1915 he accepted the post as rabbi of the Jewish Center in Manhattan, an Orthodox synagogue. But his sermons and writings made him unpopular, and in 1921 he resigned.

The next year a group of his followers helped him form his own synagogue in New York, the Society for the Advancement of Judaism. This synagogue became Kaplan's laboratory for developing his ideas about reconstructing Judaism and Jewish values. With the opening of the society in 1922, the Reconstructionist movement was born.

Kaplan gathered around him former students and rabbis who shared his views on Judaism. The synagogue bulletin, *The Reconstructionist Magazine,* was first published in 1935 and served as the voice of the new group. Kaplan's influence grew until in 1927 he faced a serious crisis.

Many of his colleagues at the seminary opposed his views, and Dr. Cyrus Adler, the seminary's president, was not pleased having Kaplan on the faculty. So Kaplan resigned. For a while he considered an offer from Dr. Stephen S. Wise who headed the new Jewish Institute of Religion founded a few years earlier. But Kaplan's deepest loyalties were with the seminary, and when his friends begged him to stay he withdrew his resignation.

Wise tried several other times to lure him away, but Kaplan could not bring himself to leave his beloved school; nor was he anxious to create a new movement which might split Jewry further apart. He still hoped that Reconstructionism would be thought of as a Jewish way of life, a philosophy that could be adopted by Jews who were Orthodox, Conservative, and Reform.

But it did not seem that this was happening, at least not rapidly enough for Kaplan's followers. In 1928 his followers urged him to form a separate party within the Conservative movement. He agreed, hoping that at least within one movement Reconstructionism would be popular. The new party set up a Reconstructionist Council and attempted to take over the Conservative Rabbinical Assembly and move it in the direction of Reconstructionism. But Kaplan always held his more radical supporters back; splitting the community was just too painful for him. He wanted to spread his ideas without official dogma, and he managed to win followers among Conservative and Reform rabbis and laypeople as well as in Zionist and secularist ranks.

All this changed in 1934 when he published his first book, *Judaism as a Civilization*. It created an explosion in Jewish life and thought. The book introduced a fully developed program for the reconstruction of Jewish theology, philosophy, ritual, and community life. It became the "Bible" of Reconstructionism. In it Kaplan presents his theory as a kind of Copernican revolution in Jewish thought. Just as Copernicus had revolutionized astronomy by arguing that the sun rather than the earth is the center of the universe, so Kaplan suggested that the Jewish people—not God—should be seen as the center of Jewish life, and everything must be done to preserve that people even if it means discarding old ideas and values while creating new ones.

Kaplan continued to write many articles and books and to teach in various colleges including the seminary and Jerusalem's Hebrew University. He very nearly decided to settle in Israel at this point in his life, but decided instead to return to America.

In 1941 Kaplan, Eugene Kohn, and Ira Eisenstein edited *The New Haggadah*, a Reconstructionist service for the Passover Seder. It was the first of many Reconstructionist prayerbooks, but it hardly prepared him for what was to come. In 1945 he edited and published a new *Sabbath Prayer Book* with the help of Kohn, Eisenstein, and Milton Steinberg. Almost immediately there was a furor in the Jewish community. Some ultra-Orthodox rabbis actually burned the new prayerbook and excommunicated Kaplan, calling him a heretic and nonbeliever. Even some of Kaplan's friends at the seminary attacked him.

Kaplan survived the attack, but felt cut off from many of the Jewish groups of which he had once been a part. He continued teaching at the Teachers Institute of the Jewish Theological Seminary of America until 1946, and the Rabbinical School of the seminary until 1963. Later he made aliyah and now lives in Jerusalem where he continues to write, lecture, and wrestle with the problems of Jewish life.

THE RECON-
STRUCTIONIST
MOVEMENT

For most of Kaplan's years of leadership of American Reconstructionism he would not allow the movement to break away from Conservative Jewry. As early as 1928 his friends had urged him to set up a national organization. This he would not do. Instead, the movement grew by setting up clubs around the country in 1935 and by establishing its own press for the publication of books, articles, and the *Reconstructionist Magazine*.

In 1940 he founded the Reconstructionist Foundation which opened its enrollment to Conservative and Reform rabbis as well as to laypeople of various Jewish groups. It was Kaplan's hope to gain supporters and to spread the teachings of Reconstructionism without creating a new split in American Jewish life. For a time the foundation was headed by Rabbi Jack Cohen, who attempted to set up a Reconstructionist Youth Fellowship. Later, in 1950, a Rabbinical Fellowship was organized and several hundred rabbis and educators joined. They were mostly "paper members," not really a part of a Reconstructionist movement, but others who felt like Kaplan that Jewish life in America required major changes to survive. The Reconstructionists also attempted to organize women's groups and youth clubs, but without great success. Reconstructionism was still not a "movement."

It was not until 1959 that Rabbi Ira Eisenstein, Kaplan's son-in-law and closest associate, formed the Fellowship of Reconstructionist Congregations. This was the break that had been expected for so long. Congregations could finally declare themselves as Reconstructionist—no longer Conservative or Reform. The movement is known today as the Federation of Reconstructionist Congregations and Fellowships and includes about forty synagogues in the United States, Central America, Canada, and Israel. The federation holds conferences and conventions, publishes books and pamphlets, and attempts to unify Reconstructionist congregations and fellowships. There are approximately three thousand families officially connected with the federation. Rabbi Ludwig Nadelman, the executive vice-president, currently runs the Reconstructionist Federation from its headquarters in New York City.

As with the mother movements, the Reconstructionists have tried to organize every aspect of their Jewish life. In 1974 the Reconstructionist Rabbinical Association was created. It now numbers fifty-one men and women. In 1968 the Reconstructionist College was founded in Philadelphia. It ordained its first rabbinical class in 1973. Its president is Rabbi Ira Eisenstein.

THE FOURTH MOVEMENT

Despite his reluctance to introduce a new, independent movement in American Jewish life, Mordecai M. Kaplan finally realized that it was the only way to spread the ideas and programs he had developed. He saw that the Jewish Theological Seminary and the Conservative movement had veered away from his ideas; and he knew that the Reform movement too was headed in a different direction. And, although many Reform and Conservative rabbis believed that Kaplan's ideas were important and called themselves Reconstructionists, he finally agreed that only a new movement with the ability to organize its own synagogues and produce its own prayer services and texts and train its own rabbis would answer his needs.

Today Reconstructionist Judaism is the fourth major movement in Jewish life. It is still small and weak compared with the three major movements, but the ideas taught by Kaplan have born fruit in every Jewish organization both here and abroad. Certainly Kaplan has earned a place as one of the great Jewish thinkers of our time. Only the future will tell how Reconstructionism will fare.

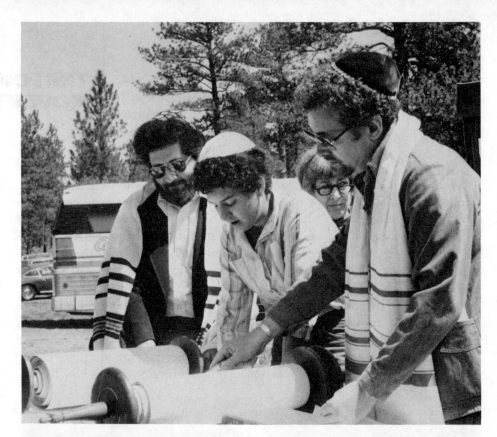

**THE RECONSTRUCTIONIST
MOVEMENT IN AMERICA**

The dream of Mordecai Kaplan was an "Organic Community," a group that would work, pray, and live together as a unit of the Jewish people. Going away together for an outdoor prayer service or meeting at one of the conventions of the Reconstructionist movement, Jews young and old come to feel this special sense of "one-ness."

The Reconstructionist Rabbinical College, founded in 1968, added new strength to the young movement. Through its classes, those studying to become rabbis can come into contact with Jewish law and tradition and with the ideas of Mordecai Kaplan. They have even been able in the recent past to come into contact with Rabbi Kaplan himself, seen on the opposite page speaking with two students. Long believing in full equality for women in Jewish life, the movement recently witnessed the simultaneous ordination of its first woman rabbi, Sandy Sasso—and her husband, Dennis.

THE RECONSTRUCTIONIST
MOVEMENT IN AMERICA

RECON-
STRUCTIONISM:
BELIEFS AND
PRACTICES

The beliefs of the other major movements have been expressed in many ways by many different scholars and thinkers. However, the major beliefs and ideas of the Reconstructionist movement come from Mordecai Kaplan's own writings and the articles published in the *Reconstructionist Magazine*. Much has been written about Reconstructionism by Rabbis Milton Steinberg, Eugene Kohn, Ira Eisenstein, and Jack Cohen, but most of Kaplan's ideas have remained basic to the movement.

A RELIGIOUS CIVILIZATION

The most important of these teachings is that Judaism is a changing, evolving, developing *religious civilization*. In biblical times, Jews formed a *people*. Later, we became a *religious congregation*, a people that prayed and worshipped together. Then we entered the *rabbinic* era, when the rules of the sages and halachah controlled our lives. Now we have entered the democratic era and we live as Jews because we choose to do so. Our lives are no longer controlled by Jewish law or the Jewish people. Naturally, our ideas about God, humanity, sin, miracles, Jewish law, the world, prayer, and life after death have changed as each of these periods has changed.

Kaplan calls us a "religious civilization" because he feels that religion is the special ingredient that gives our lives meaning. According to Kaplan, religion is necessary to any people and culture because it raises us above the animals, helps us to fulfill ourselves as human beings, and makes our lives holy. As important as religion is, however, it is only one part of a whole civilization. Kaplan views Judaism as much more than worship of God, prayer, and the performance of mitzvot. The Jewish people have created their own art, music, language, folkways, and customs. In short, Judaism is not only a religion, but a total civilization.

But what is the purpose of a special Jewish civilization? Kaplan answers that Jewish civilization is built in such a way—made up of Torah, religion, customs, and culture—as to insure the creative survival of the Jewish people. Clearly, the Jewish peoplehood is at the heart of the Reconstructionist movement. And this definition of the Jewish people today as a religious civilization has been accepted even by Jews who are not Reconstructionists.

RECONSTRUC-TIONISM AND THE OTHER MOVEMENTS

Reconstructionism recognizes that each of the major movements has made important contributions to the Jewish people, but at the same time is critical of them. For example, the Reconstructionists admire Orthodoxy because it insists on maximum Jewish education and it inspires its members to make great sacrifices for their beliefs. But the Reconstructionists feel that Orthodoxy relies too much on the supernatural—believing in a personal God and miracles—to appeal to modern Jews. Reform is important because it is concerned about the need for growth and change in Jewish law and life, but it can be criticized because it neglects the religious meaning of the Jewish peoplehood and the value of ritual. Conservative Judaism maintains the importance of a vital Jewish peoplehood, but it is too concerned with the past and with its attempts to remain true to halachah while changing halachah. Its attempts to modernize the Jewish law are painfully slow and needlessly difficult. Zionism is important because of its passion for Eretz Yisrael, but it has overlooked the needs of the Jews who live in the *Diaspora* (countries other than Israel). Secularism (the belief that Judaism can survive without religion) misses the mark because it fails to see the importance of religious expression, though it is important because it believes in the development of Jewish art and culture.

Since each of these philosophies has serious shortcomings, the best hope, according to the Reconstructionists, is a *reconstruction* of Jewish ideas, life, and philosophy. And that is the essence of Mordecai Kaplan's approach. The seal of the Reconstructionist movement explains its basic goals. The form is that of a wheel. The hub of the wheel is Israel, the center of Jewish civilization from which all the important forces of Judaism radiate. Religion, culture, and ethics are the spokes of the wheel by which the vital influence of Israel is felt on Jewish life everywhere and which enables Israel to make its special contribution to the civilization of the world. The wheel has an inner and an outer rim. The inner rim represents the Jewish community tied to Israel even though it is dispersed throughout the world. It is attached to Israel by bonds of religion, ethics, and culture. The outer rim is the general community, for us the community of America, with which the Jewish civilization maintains contact at every point. The seal thus symbolizes the whole philosophy of the Reconstructionist movement.

GOD

Mordecai Kaplan's ideas about God are untraditional. Kaplan is a "humanist-naturalist." He is a humanist because he finds God in people and in human experience. Our potential and our striving to do better, to reach higher, to achieve greater things, and to rise above the lowly animals reflects the power of God. And Kaplan also finds evidence of God in the universe and in nature because the universe has order and laws, rules and design. Nature's order is designed to help us to achieve our highest goals. In this way, Kaplan believes that we must found our belief in God on modern, scientific, and rational facts and on a faith in humanity and in the universe as having the elements we need for raising our own moral and ethical behavior.

Kaplan defines God as the power or process that makes for human salvation and fulfillment, for the realization of the "highest ideals for which men strive." Basically, Kaplan has a deep faith that people (and the universe of which people are part) have in them a force or power driving them to reach for ideals such as justice and truth, goodness and peace. Just as gravity is a power in nature which cannot be seen but is always felt, so there is a power in human beings and in the world that makes us search for betterment and fulfillment. That power is what we call "God."

Reconstructionism does not teach that God is a person living in heaven and writing our deeds in a book. That concept, says Kaplan, is silly, childlike *supernaturalism*. We can't see or feel God and we should not try to. Nor should we try to know God through mystical experiences. Even the belief in miracles seems childish and primitive since modern science has taught us that the laws and dynamics of the universe cannot be suspended or stopped. Therefore we should not think of God as a miracle-worker. Nor should we think of God as a judge who will reward or punish us in the next life. Our concern should be for *this* world, not the next. We are expected to live the good life here and now. The idea of a God who will reward or punish in some next life is just not a modern way of thinking, according to Kaplan.

In the library of the Reconstructionist Rabbinical College, students can keep up with what's happening on the world scene, even as they continue their studies of the Jewish past.

But the most radical change in the way Kaplan thinks about God is his idea that God's power is limited. For if God were all powerful, how could He allow evil and suffering in the world? The Reconstructionists believe that there are things that are within God's power and things that God cannot control, at least not now. For God's holiness has not yet filled the world. That part of life and the world not yet filled with God's presence is what we call "evil." We must have faith that someday God's spirit will fill the entire world and evil and suffering will disappear. Our task as human beings and as Jews is to bring that day ever closer.

With the exception of Rabbi Milton Steinberg, Reconstructionist thinkers have accepted these ideas about God. Steinberg felt that Kaplan's definition of God was too cold and rationalistic. He wanted to think of God as more than just a power or process; he longed for some mystery in religion because he felt that life itself contains some mystery and wonder. But most Reconstructionists have sided with Kaplan.

TORAH

Reconstructionism differs greatly from traditional Judaism because it does not believe that God revealed the Torah to Moses at Sinai. The Reconstructionists accept the thinking of modern biblical scholars who teach that the Bible is the work of many people in many ages. Kaplan wrote that the Bible is not the record of God's word to us but of our search for God. Whenever we discover a religious truth or great moral idea, it is for us a revelation of God's will.

Because of this view about the giving of Torah, Reconstructionists do not believe that the halachah is holy and unchangeable and do not speak in terms of mitzvot. They point out that since the Jewish community can no longer enforce observance of Jewish law and since each Jew can now *choose* to keep the law as he or she sees fit, it is foolish to use the old terms "halachah" and "mitzvot." The Reconstructionists instead call the mitzvot "folkways" and "customs." Every people in history has created its own folkways and customs; each civilization has its heroes, sacred events, holy days, and holy objects. In the same way, Judaism has its heroes—Moses, Akiba, Rashi, Maimonides— its sacred events—birth, marriage, Bar and Bat Mitzvah—its holy days— Sabbath, Rosh Hashanah, Yom Kippur—and its holy objects—Torah. These folkways and customs bring us closer to God and help us to lead more meaningful lives. But even more importantly, they bind us together as a people and keep the Jewish people alive and flourishing. So we need not observe rituals such as Sabbath because God commanded us to do so and they are mitzvot or law, but because observing Sabbath teaches us the importance of rest and helps us to survive as one people by uniting us.

A RECON-STRUCTIONIST GUIDE TO RITUAL

Kaplan hoped that the customs that help preserve the historic chain of the Jewish people and that enrich our spiritual lives might be preserved. But he taught that these should be accepted willingly by the people; no one should be forced to observe a custom. He supported the idea of a democratic vote by which people might decide which laws they would keep or not keep. And, while he taught that the tradition should always be consulted before laws were changed, he felt that the past alone should not decide for us: "The past should have a vote, not a veto."

Kaplan also taught that mitzvot that seemed out of date or clashed with our highest ideals should be reinterpreted. If no new meanings could be found in them, they should be dropped. Of course this privilege to change the past also carries with it the responsibility for us to create new customs and practices to replace the old. Kaplan was in the forefront of this trend. He worked for women's liberation within Jewish life long before we used the words "women's liberation." He created the Bat Mitzvah ceremony for girls in order to give them a feeling of equality in Jewish ritual life.

At first it was thought that giving each individual the right to choose personally meaningful rituals might lead to chaos. But Kaplan suggested that this problem might be avoided by creating guides to Jewish living that a person would be free to follow or to reject. Such a *Guide to Ritual Usage* was prepared in 1941. It outlines practices that might help a Jew to survive as a Jew and to grow spiritually. But above all, the people and not the rabbis, Kaplan taught, must have the final say in accepting or dropping mitzvot. Indeed, in Kaplan's congregation, the Society for the Advancement of Judaism, the entire membership votes for or against ritual changes. This may be one reason the Reconstructionist movement is the most democratic of all Jewish groups.

THE JEWISH PEOPLE

Reconstructionism places its heaviest emphasis on *Am Yisrael*, the Jewish people, which is the center of Jewish civilization. The purpose of the civilization is to keep the Jewish people alive and vibrant, that is, to create values that give worth to human life. Furthermore, the Torah exists for the sake of the Jewish people since it is a cornerstone of Jewish civilization. Kaplan wrote that it is a great mitzvah for any people to survive, create, and flourish; it is a particularly great mitzvah for Jews to live as a "people created in the image of God." He felt strongly that we must revive the Jewish people's will to live and

Although Reconstructionist ideas of God differ greatly from those of the Orthodox, the movement believes in keeping as much as possible of traditional observance. Here, Rabbis Kaplan and Eisenstein take part in the Sukkot ritual of lulav and etrog.

create. In fact, he suggested that representatives of world Jewry gather together in Jerusalem to renew formally the brit (covenant) of Sinai.

Kaplan did not call the Jewish people a "chosen people." He thought this a racist notion because it seems to say that we are a superior race. Agreeing with Kaplan, Rabbi Eugene Kohn wrote that calling the Jewish people "chosen" suggests that other peoples are "rejected." Most Reconstructionists agree that in a democratic time like ours, it is boastful to speak of a chosen people. Jews should try to drop any idea that we are "superior" to other peoples. So the term "chosen people" has been taken out of all Reconstructionist prayerbooks and rituals.

In place of the idea of chosenness, Kaplan taught the Reform idea of "Mission." He wrote, "The purpose of Jewish existence is to foster in ourselves as Jews, and to awaken in the rest of the world, a sense of moral responsibility in action. . . . When that comes about, the Messianic Age will have arrived."

Reconstructionists understand that a Jew's only choice is to live in two civilizations at once. American Jews live both in the American civilization and in the Jewish civilization. Even Israeli Jews must live in Israeli civilization at the same time they live in Jewish civilization. It is the job of Jews to borrow the best from both civilizations, to strengthen the Jewish civilization, and to blend the two into a happy combination.

Kaplan had been a Zionist from his youth and his followers are all devoted Zionists. By and large, Reconstructionists believe that a full Jewish life is possible only in Eretz Yisrael; in fact, Kaplan and many of his students have actually settled in Israel. But Kaplan was realistic, too. He knew that all Jewish communities around the world would not disappear, that all Jews would not move to Israel. So he rejected the standard Zionist idea that all Jews must make aliyah. He also opposed the Orthodox view that Israel must be a Torah state run according to halachah without separation of religion and government.

THE LAND OF ISRAEL

In issuing a call for a "new Zionism," Kaplan borrowed the ideas of the Russian-Zionist thinker Ahad Ha'am who had suggested that Eretz Yisrael must be a cultural and spiritual center that would guide world Jewry. Kaplan hoped that the new state of Israel would achieve that goal and that Israel and world Jewry would influence and enrich one another. Nevertheless, Kaplan taught that Israel should be based on religious and moral principles. "Before the Torah can go forth from Zion," he wrote "it will have to enter into Zionism." Zionism is a means to a higher goal: the revival of the spirit of the Jewish people. Only a creative partnership between Israel and the Jewish people throughout the world could do this.

In the early part of the twentieth century Mordecai Kaplan helped organize New York's *kehillah*. It was a part of his dream to unify the Jewish community and bring together all Jewish groups and organizations and thereby strengthen Jewry. He never lost sight of that goal. He continually urged Jews to set up "organic communities" such as the kehillot of Europe, but communities in which membership would be voluntary and not forced. These American kehillot would include Jewish community councils or organizations to which all Jews and Jewish groups would be encouraged to belong regardless of religious or political differences. Kaplan proposed that an ideal organic community do the following:

THE JEWISH COMMUNITY

1. Keep records of vital statistics
2. Encourage Jews to join local and national Jewish organizations
3. Set a budget for Jewish organizations to spend on Jewish needs
4. Develop guidelines of ethical and moral behavior
5. Strengthen Jewish education and culture
6. Work to improve the health and welfare of Jews and to eliminate poverty within the Jewish community
7. Encourage culture and the arts
8. Fight discrimination and anti-Semitism
9. Work with non-Jewish groups for the common good

Although Jewish community councils have been set up in many communities in America, Kaplan's dream of organic communities has not yet been fulfilled.

SOCIAL ACTION

In much the same way, Kaplan taught that the goal of religion is to bring salvation or fulfillment to the group and not just to the individual. This could happen if the religious principles and beliefs were translated into ethical and moral action. So the Reconstructionist movement has been involved in social issues from the start. In the 1930s Kaplan and Eisenstein supported the socialist idea that the government should control major industries in America and that the cruel competition of private business should be ended. More recently, the movement has supported labor unions in their struggle to make working conditions better, fought for civil rights, and supported more liberal laws of birth control and abortion. It is a defender of the United Nations and works for world disarmament. It has opposed the death penalty.

In the past the movement has also opposed government aid for private and parochial schools. In fact, Kaplan opposed sending children to yeshivot and parochial schools because he believed that such education was undemocratic and separated children from the American society. In recent years he has changed his position and now agrees that parochial school and yeshivah education can be helpful to Jewish children, at least in the lower grades. Still a supporter of the public school system, he proposed that American history and government be taught in public schools as a kind of civic "religion," with special attention given to the ethics of freedom and justice. In short, he believes that both the American and Jewish communities would be strengthened if democracy would be considered a kind of public faith.

INTERFAITH ACTIVITIES

Oddly, Reconstructionism has not been too active in interfaith activities. Rabbi Kaplan believed that religious debates and dialogues could seldom succeed since most religions consider themselves superior to other religions and friendly discussion often becomes impossible. Rabbi Ira Eisenstein has also been cautious about such activities because he feels that as long as each religion claims that it alone has the only truth, cooperation is an impossible dream. But Reconstructionist leaders do try to work together with other Jews and non-Jews on problems of a nonreligious nature such as the fight against poverty and disease, oppression and corruption.

RELIGIOUS PRACTICES

Because of their belief that mitzvot can be changed or even dropped, the religious practices of the Reconstructionists differ from congregation to congregation, from place to place. The movement believes that Jews observe some rituals in order to enrich their lives spiritually and strengthen their ties to the Jewish people. But the choice of which to observe is left to the individual and the congregation; and the movement tries not to use any force or to speak of sin or guilt. Dr. Kaplan has remained throughout his life an observant Jew: he prays daily, keeps kosher, observes Sabbath and festivals. But many of his followers are not nearly so observant.

Although the movement has published a *Guide to Ritual Usage,* it is merely a guide. The individual is free to follow or not follow it. For example, the *Guide* states that on the Sabbath one may do things not possible the rest of the week as "a way of enjoying life." For some people this means going to synagogue, refraining from work, and studying Torah. But for others this may mean playing golf or tennis or sailing. Some keep the Sabbath carefully and others do not. Kashrut is officially favored by the movement, because—as Kaplan wrote—it teaches us that we eat to live, not live to eat, and it raises the animal act of eating to a holy act. But Kaplan suggested that if keeping kosher away from home is too difficult and requires too great a sacrifice, then the Reconstructionist may eat nonkosher foods. Many Reconstructionists will keep kosher at home and eat nonkosher when away from home.

Reconstructionists believe firmly in marriage within the faith. They use a ketubah but do not insist on a get. Their children are circumcised and named in traditional fashion and some new ceremonies for the naming of girls have recently appeared. Bar and Bat Mitzvah are important milestones in a Reconstructionist life, and the movement tries to provide good Jewish education for the children of its members, stressing Hebrew, Israel, ethics, and thought. Burial and mourning rituals differ greatly from place to place depending on how traditional the mourners are and what practices they choose to observe.

THE RECON-STRUCTIONIST SYNAGOGUE-CENTER

Dr. Kaplan originated the idea of a synagogue-center that would provide religious, cultural, charitable, social, and athletic activities for its members. His idea was quite popular and, in fact, many American synagogues of all movements have become synagogue-centers. The synagogue-center grew out of the idea that Judaism is a religious civilization and must provide for Jews all the activities of a civilization as well as those of a religion.

Within the synagogue, the Reconstructionists have been creative in their worship services. Musical instruments and choirs are often used, community singing is popular, and men and women sit together. Men are required to wear yarmulkes and talit. The old differences between the priestly classes (Kohen and Levi) and the people (Israel) have been removed to make the synagogue more democratic. The prayerbooks have been specially edited to speak in Reconstructionist terms. Most of the prayers are in Hebrew since it is felt that Hebrew is an important part of the Jewish civilization. But many of the traditional Hebrew prayers have been changed and modern prayers both in Hebrew and English have been added. The second days of the festivals have been dropped by most Reconstructionist synagogues, just as they have been omitted by Reform and some Conservative synagogues.

The movement has been open to experimenting with new rituals and practices, to creating new customs and dropping old ones. Often such changes are brought about by majority vote of the members of a congregation. Of all the religious movements in American Jewry, Reconstructionism is the one least tied to tradition, least concerned with past practices, and most ready to change, create, and innovate.

THE NEW HAGGADAH

הַגָּדָה שֶׁל פֶּסַח סֵדֶר חָדָשׁ

Among the many liturgical works of the Reconstructionists, The New Haggadah, first published in 1942 and revised in 1978, has been the most popular. It is widely used even by Reform and Conservative Jews.

JEWISH MYSTICISM AND HASIDISM

VARIATIONS ON A THEME

You may be surprised at the many different ways in which Jews express their religion today. Visitors from the Jewish past — Moses, Rashi, Maimonides, and others — would be shocked. It has been many centuries since Jewish thinkers differed on so many basic ideas and values, customs and rituals. Not only are there four major varieties of Judaism from which a Jew may choose, there are other minor variations on the theme of Judaism, too. These are not truly separate movements, but spinoffs from the larger groups. Because we are concerned here with religious movements, we will not deal with such movements as Zionism and secularism, but it is worthwhile to study some of the religious spinoffs, particularly mysticism and Hasidism.

MYSTICISM

Mysticism is not new to Jewish life. In the Middle Ages it was known as *kabbalah* and was popular among small groups of scholars in many countries. Two hundred years ago many of its ideas were taken over and popularized by the Hasidic movement in Poland, Galicia, and Austria. Yet mysticism continued to exist separately from the Hasidic movement and alongside the mainstream of traditional Jewish life.

Mysticism teaches that God can be known through inner experiences and personal encounters. Such experiences can hardly be expressed in writing, they have to be felt. And not everyone can feel them; one must first prepare for the experience. Preparing means studying texts, doing special

A Jewish scribe carefully corrects faded or damaged letters to make this much-used Torah scroll kosher **again**. The mystics say that in the World to Come we will learn to read not only the letters and the words of the Torah, but even the white spaces between them.

kinds of exercises, and being taught by other mystics.

Because Americans in general have recently become more interested in the religions of the Far East, many of which are devoted to mysticism and mystical experience, a new interest in mysticism has been growing among American Jews—especially among the young. There may be other reasons for this new interest, too—Jewish reasons. The tragic wars of the past forty years, the Holocaust, the agony of racial conflicts, and the uncertainty of Jewish life in modern times have caused many Jews to lose faith in rationalism (the use of logic and reason), science, and traditional religion. Some have lost faith in humanity and believe that truth can be found only in mystical experience. Many seek strong spiritual leaders, powerful religious personalities to whom they can turn for guidance and absolute answers to their problems.

And scholars have turned their attention to mysticism, too. Such important Jewish thinkers as Martin Buber, Gershom Scholem, and Abraham Joshua Heschel have studied the history and texts of Jewish mysticism and through their writings made these known to Jews around the world.

ABRAHAM JOSHUA HESCHEL

The most brilliant and respected teacher of mystical thought for the modern Jew was Professor Abraham Joshua Heschel. Heschel came from a famous Hasidic family, was educated in Poland and Germany, and taught at the Jewish Theological Seminary until his death in 1973. Although he was known as a Conservative Jew, his interpretation of Judaism based on mysticism had an influence on all Jewish movements.

Heschel wrote in a beautiful, poetic way. He defined Judaism as the answer to our most important questions and a response to the mystery of life.

What we have learned from Jewish history is that if a man is not more than human then he is less than human. Judaism is an attempt to prove that in order to be a man, you have to be more than a man, that in order to be a people we have to be more than a people. Israel was made to be a "holy people." This is the essence of its merit. Judaism is a link to eternity, kinship with ultimate reality. —

Heschel taught that Judaism is a religion of *time* rather than *space;* events in time such as Shabbat or Bar Mitzvah are more important than places or buildings. He believed that following a creed or list of principles was less important than believing from the depths of our being and accepting the demands of Judaism, including a faith in God, Torah, and Israel.

According to Heschel, it is unnecessary and impossible to prove that God exists. Along with the mystics he taught that we can see God's power in the mysteries of nature and history; in the starry heavens above and in the moral order on earth. We need not express that sense of mystery aloud, it is enough if we are amazed by it. We cannot hope to fully understand the reality of God, but we can approach God through our prayers, through a study of God's Torah, and through observing God's mitzvot.

Heschel kept the mitzvot but not in an Orthodox way. He disapproved of the Orthodox who observe mitzvot in an automatic way without heart and soul and who have made Jewish law a mass of prohibitions and "thou shalt nots." He thought it wrong to believe that Judaism is concerned only with what we *do*. Judaism calls upon us, first of all, to be a holy people; and so it is calling upon us to develop *kavannah;* the inner spirit, and a way of thinking, not just a way of living. He used the Sabbath as an example:

> *Perhaps Sabbath is the idea that expresses what is most characteristic of Judaism.*
>
> *What is the Sabbath? A reminder of every man's royalty; an abolition of the distinction of master and slave, rich and poor, success and failure. To celebrate the Sabbath is to experience one's ultimate independence of civilization and society, of achievement and anxiety. The Sabbath is an embodiment of the belief that all men are equal and that equality of men means the nobility of men. The greatest sin of man is to forget that he is a prince.*
>
> *The Sabbath is an assurance that the spirit is greater than the universe, that beyond the good is the holy. The universe was created in six days, but the climax of creation was the seventh day. Things that come into being in the six days are good, but the seventh day is holy. The Sabbath is holiness in time.*

All mystics believe that what we do here on earth can affect what happens in heaven, and Heschel taught that God needs us even as we need God. He believed that revelation, the giving of the Law and the making of the brit at Sinai, occurred but once—a dialogue between God and us. Now human beings must continue to interpret God's words, developing halachah and mitzvot.

He wrote a good deal about prayer, too, for the mystics place great value on prayer. Heschel knew that many people feel embarrassed about speaking to God through prayer, but taught that God does listen to prayer and that we must learn to trust our inner spirit as we pray. Others should not be allowed to pray for us. In his final public statement on television, he called on young people to sharpen their sensitivity toward the mysteries of life and to celebrate sacred moments and express their joy.

Heschel called the Jewish people a holy people whose task it is to be more than a people, to be a religious order. He was devoted to the land of Israel and wrote about it as the Kabbalists of old had written, "Israel reborn is holy." There is a mystic bond between world Jewry reborn and Eretz Yisrael, he said, and "there can be no wholeness outside of Israel."

Not only was he a mystic, but Heschel's mysticism included an active interest in the affairs of our times. He spoke out against racism, calling it "a cancer of the soul," and he marched with Martin Luther King, Jr. in support of equal civil rights for blacks. He warned against letting religion become a formal institution which might lose sight of the people, and suggested that Judaism must teach that it is evil not to care about the fate of others. He was in favor of dialogues and discussions with people of other faiths, and was an adviser to the Vatican as the Catholic Church worked to form a new attitude toward Judaism.

Heschel did not create a separate Judaic movement, but he introduced mystical ideas and Hasidic thought to the American public in a beautiful and inspiring way. Even Christian thinkers have studied his speeches and writings. Judaism will long feel his influence.

MYSTICISM TODAY

Mysticism continues to be studied and taught in many major universities throughout the United States and often in synagogues as well. Small groups of mystics meet together from time to time and some have even formed small societies. But for the most part mystics have been happy as members of the four major religious movements and have not tried to unite as a separate movement. This may be because the mystical experience is so personal that no group could hope to describe or interpret it. Even individuals who are mystics often have trouble telling of their mystical experiences, and this is one reason studying Heschel—who wrote, spoke, and lived his mysticism for all to understand—is a good way of understanding the mystical experience.

HASIDISM

Hasidism began with the Baal Shem Tov who lived in eastern Europe in the eighteenth century. It soon became a popular movement, almost a "folk" movement, and its membership in east Europe grew steadily until the Second World War. Through the years the original Hasidic movement split into many small groups, each following a *tzaddik* or "saint," each believing that their tzaddik was more powerful than any other. Hasidism took many of the ideas of medieval mysticism and taught them in a simple way, through legends and stories, to uneducated and oppressed Jews. Even today we continue to marvel in these stories, finding in them much which is useful and inspirational.

The centers of Hasidism are here in the United States and in Israel. In truth Hasidism cannot be said to be one movement; it is a group of small movements each with its own teachings. But to understand it and the way it is today, perhaps the best group to study is the Lubavitch group which makes its headquarters in Brooklyn, New York.

THE LUBAVITCHER REBBE

The Lubavitch Hasidic movement is the largest Hasidic group in the United States. Founded in Russia around 1800, Lubavitcher Hasidism is the most intellectual of the Hasidic sects. Its motto is *hochmah* (wisdom), *binah* (understanding), and *daat* (knowledge). Using the first three letters of the motto the movement is often called simply *HaBaD*. The present tzaddik, or *rebbe*, of the movement is Rabbi Menahem Schneerson, who was born in Russia in 1902, studied both in secular and traditional Torah subjects, and came to America in 1941. He is known as the *Lubavitcher Rebbe*. His headquarters in Brooklyn is a spiritual center for his many followers and he has had a tremendous influence on Hasidism here and throughout the world.

The Rebbe has not published any formal works of philosophy, but his lectures, letters, sermons, and brief commentaries have been widely studied. He has tried to blend Hasidism with modern thought, although his approach is far more Orthodox and traditional than Heschel's and his views are simple. The Rebbe wrote that the entire Torah is holy and no part of it is unimportant. He insisted that there is no conflict between science and Judaism:

> *He who says that science contradicts religion is talking rubbish. True science is highly compatible with faith. . . . The Torah is truth, and science is truth, therefore there can exist no conflict between the two. In fact, the findings of the past few years confirm what is said in the Torah —ideas which scientists a generation ago would not have believed.*

But the Rebbe does not always agree with science. For example, he does not accept Darwin's theory of evolution or the geological finding that the world is millions of years old. He believes that the fossils that have been discovered by anthropologists and geologists are not from a prehistoric era, but were placed on earth by God at the time of creation, some fifty-seven hundred years ago.

The Lubavitcher Rebbe's Hasidism is practical; it is based on his belief in Torah learning and religious spirit. He has organized campaigns to encourage Jews to perform such mitzvot as lighting the candles for Sabbath and holidays, kashrut, the daily wearing of tefillin, and the placing of a mezuzah on the doorpost. He has sent his followers out in "mitzvah tanks," vans loaded with pamphlets and materials, to bring the Lubavitcher message to various Jewish neighborhoods, and his "missionaries" have traveled to many parts of the world to set up yeshivot and synagogues. Yet the Rebbe, who is modern enough to think of an idea like the mitzvah tank, is still rooted in tradition when

The Lubavitcher Rebbe sends "missionaries" throughout the world to bring Jews back to their traditional roots. Here, one of his missionaries conducts a study session for women in St. Paul, Minnesota.

it comes to current issues such as women's rights. He has written that women are more emotional than intellectual, that their function is different from men's, and that they should concentrate on strictly female mitzvot such as mikveh, lighting Sabbath candles, and raising children. He is strongly opposed to the use of birth control and to abortion.

Recalling an idea of the Reform movement, the Rebbe believes in the Jewish "Mission." He wrote that God has scattered our people around the world to bring the message of Torah to every corner of the globe and to teach the idea of monotheism to all human beings. He looks to Israel as the model of Torah law in action, but actually the Rebbe has been troubled by the secularism of Israel's government. He believes that today it would be easier than ever to conduct the nation of Israel in keeping with traditional halachah since modern technology and science has increased productivity and we can now afford to rest on the Sabbath and festivals. And he has called on Israel to follow Torah principles; not to be a secular state, but a state where religion and government are one.

In theory the Lubavitcher group believes that one should love any Jew, even one who does not keep the mitzvot. Yet the Rebbe wrote a letter forbidding his followers to work together with non-Orthodox Jews in community organizations such as the Synagogue Council of America or the local Board of Rabbis. He explained that it is a sin to cooperate with heretics and nonbelievers, as he calls Reform and Conservative Jews. So there has been little Hasidic involvement in community affairs and little in the area of social action, except on matters that affect the Orthodox community. For example, Hasidim favor government aid to parochial schools because their yeshivot are in serious financial difficulties. They have also fought politically against racial redistricting of their communities since they believe that this would cut their political power. But generally, the Lubavitcher group has not been interested in interfaith or interreligious activities.

Obviously the Lubavitcher sect led by its rebbe has set itself both limits and goals. It has been successful in bringing the teachings of Hasidic Orthodoxy to a wide circle of people. Its rebbe has been successful in using modern advertising methods to spread his teachings and the group's ideas, and the growing number of American-born Hasidim can be traced mainly to the efforts of the Lubavitcher group.

AMERICAN JUDAISM TODAY: AN OVERVIEW

Now that we have studied how the various movements came to be and what they believe in and how they practice Judaism today, it would be helpful to try to see the community as a whole. Here is a short summary of the major movements that we have studied, along with some of the strengths of each movement's ideas.

ORTHODOXY

1. Orthodoxy teaches that God is a supernatural, superhuman being who performs miracles, hears prayer, knows our thoughts and actions, and is all-powerful, all-good, all-present, and all-wise.

2. The Torah is totally God's word as revealed at Sinai and is binding on us for all times. The interpretations of the sages in the Talmud and law codes are also binding and also part of Torah. Halachah and mitzvot are the basic parts of Judaism and may be reinterpreted only by great sages. Orthodox Jews must observe as many of the 613 commandments as possible without questioning God's will. Judaism must not change with every passing fashion, but must preserve the tradition from generation to generation in order that our people may survive.

3. Synagogue worship and prayers must not be changed. Jewish children should receive a yeshivah education, wherever possible, with stress on the Talmud and Bible.

4. The Jewish people are chosen by God to keep the mitzvot and spread God's word to the world. The Orthodox believe theirs is the only correct version of Judaism and that other movements and beliefs are dangerous and even sinful.

5. The state of Israel is the holy land of the Jewish people and must be

built on the foundations of the Torah, tradition, and halachah. It is the means to spiritual revival for world Jewry and Jewish law.

6. Orthodoxy is willing to cooperate with other Jewish groups on certain issues (especially those that concern Orthodox interests), but lately has been uninterested in any great amount of cooperation.

7. Orthodoxy has not been overly involved in social action except in areas of Jewish interest or where Orthodox goals are at stake.

8. The Orthodox generally opposes interfaith activities and views them as leading only to conversion.

FACTS TO REMEMBER

1. Orthodoxy presents a simple, firm, clear-cut faith.

2. Since it believes that the entire Torah is the word of God, it is easy for an Orthodox Jew to know precisely what is required, to observe the mitzvot without questioning.

3. Orthodoxy has succeeded in inspiring its people to make great sacrifices. Orthodox Jews are practically the only ones who observe the mitzvot precisely. Indeed, the traditional concepts of Sabbath, Yom Tov, kashrut, and synagogue worship would be endangered except for Orthodoxy.

4. The Orthodox community has taught the value of maximum Jewish education through its many yeshivot.

5. Orthodoxy has given Jews a strong tie to tradition and to the Jewish past.

1. Reform teaches that Judaism is an evolving religion that must continue to change in order to meet the needs of our time.

2. Many different ideas of God are accepted, ranging from the Orthodox to the most scientific and liberal.

3. Only the ethical mitzvot of the Torah were revealed by God and are forever binding. Ritual laws were developed by human beings to satisfy the needs of their days. These laws may be changed with each passing generation in order to raise our spiritual level and unite our people.

Following mitzvot is a matter of individual choice. Each person must consult his or her own conscience, or may refer to guides to observance for help.

4. Prayer, worship, and the language of the prayerbook must change in each generation to fill the needs of the Jewish people.

5. The Jewish people are a spiritual people whose mission is to teach monotheism and morality to the world.

6. The land of Israel must be the spiritual-moral center of world Jewry, but religion and the state should be separated in Israel.

7. Social action, concern for others, especially in the spirit of Israel's prophets, is at the heart of Judaism's message and must be practiced by every Jew.

8. Reform is deeply involved in interfaith work and is convinced that this is the best way to wipe out religious prejudice.

REFORM JUDAISM

1. Reform is dynamic, changing, always open to new ideas and views.

2. The too-often neglected ethical core of Judaism has been rediscovered by Reform.

3. Reform has taught Jews that they can live in this world, deal with secular challenges and problems, be part of the community, and still remain Jews.

4. Reform is always willing to experiment with new practices, ceremonies, and rituals to strengthen Jewish living.

FACTS TO REMEMBER

CONSERVATIVE JUDAISM

1. Judaism is viewed as a changing religious civilization.

2. Conservatism seeks to balance tradition and change, the teachings of the past with the needs of the present and the future.

3. The main purpose of Judaism is to preserve the Jewish people.

4. The Conservative movement accepts Torah as the revealed word of God, but not in the literal sense. Conservatism teaches that human beings have played a role in interpreting Torah and so Torah and Jewish law have grown and changed throughout history. It urges that halachah must be constantly reinterpreted in the light of changing ethical, social, and economic needs. While Conservatism favors tradition and expects its members to observe mitzvot, it is willing to adjust certain ritual laws.

5. The synagogue is considered the basic Jewish institution (aside from the Jewish home, of course). The synagogue must serve the many needs of Jews. Its prayers and worship service must be updated but with reverence for Hebrew and tradition. Maximum Jewish education, including day schools and Hebrew high schools, is encouraged.

6. The Jewish people form one united body and should unite as one world community.

7. Israel is the holy land and should be the spiritual-cultural center of world Jewry. It is a mitzvah to aid Israel and to settle there. But Conservative Jewry calls on the state of Israel to separate religion from government.

8. Social action for civil and human rights is important.

9. Interfaith dialogue and study among scholars and thinkers should be encouraged because it helps to promote peace, understanding, and harmony.

FACTS TO REMEMBER

1. Conservatism properly places stress on the centrality of the Jewish people and their need to survive creatively.

2. The Conservative movement strikes a balance between tradition and change, old and new, ritual and ethics.

3. Conservatism modernizes through careful change rather than rash revolution.

4. Because Conservatism is not an extreme philosophy, it appeals to the majority of American Jews.

1. Judaism is viewed as an evolving, changing religious civilization that has always been developing and is now in the age of democracy and free choice.

2. Reconstructionism believes that Jewish civilization exists to maintain the creative survival of the Jewish people.

3. Jewish values must be reinterpreted to insure and promote our creative survival.

4. God is a natural power or process, not a supernatural being. God is the power that makes for human salvation. Our idea of God must come from experience rather than thought.

5. The Torah is not considered the revealed word of God by Reconstructionists, but the record of our search for God's presence in our world. Jews are no longer bound by halachah and mitzvot, and only those customs or folkways that enrich our spiritual lives and unite us as a people are important. The people have the right to choose their observances by democratic means.

6. The synagogue must be a center for all Jewish activities and prayers must be constantly changed as we change our ethical and religious ideas and beliefs.

7. Reconstructionism rejects the idea that Jews are the chosen people, but it expects Jews to live up to their mission as a people created in God's image.

8. Reconstructionism wants Eretz Yisrael to be the spiritual center of world Jewry and to enrich world Jewry with new ethical and religious inspiration.

9. World Jewish communities should organize into "organic" communities and strengthen and enrich one another.

10. Social action is at the heart of Judaism's message and must be supported by all Jews.

11. Interfaith activities too often lead to anger or competition and should be avoided except when everyone's well-being is at stake.

RECONSTRUCTIONIST JUDAISM

FACTS TO REMEMBER

1. Reconstructionism rightly speaks of the need to help the Jewish people survive creatively.

2. Reconstructionism has a proper respect for tradition without being enslaved by it; and it teaches the need for people to have a large role in deciding how they will observe their faith.

3. Reconstructionism is based on natural, human experience familiar to us all, rather than on ancient texts alone.

4. Reconstructionism reinterprets ancient values in the light of the present.

5. Reconstructionism reminds us of the need to live in two civilizations at once and to be enriched by both.

6. Reconstructionism has been a valuable goad to our thinking and has helped us to shake old myths.

IN CONCLUSION

American Judaism has come a long way in a short three hundred years. In America today there are about six million Jews; more than three thousand rabbis and almost four thousand synagogues; seminaries and yeshivot; native-born scholars; four hundred thousand children in religious schools including more than eighty thousand students attending the hundreds of all-day schools for intensive Jewish education. Thousands study Hebrew language in high schools and colleges; thousands take adult study courses in congregation and Jewish colleges; thousands are enrolled in youth groups and in Jewish or Hebrew-speaking camps; and thousands visit or study in Israel each year.

Today it is easier than ever to keep kosher and observe the Sabbath and holidays—at least in the major centers of Jewish life—and many Jews do so. It was unheard of to find a yarmulke on a college student in a secular university twenty years ago, and an observant college professor was a great rarity. Today these are commonplace. Despite the many problems of American Jewry—the high rate of mixed marriage, widespread Jewish illiteracy, a low birth rate, and rapidly decaying Jewish neighborhoods in the inner cities—we have made great progress since the first generation of immigrants came here a little more than three centuries ago.

And a greater variety of Jewish beliefs and experiences is found in this country than in any other land or at any other time in Jewish history. We have discussed and compared the four main religious movements and two minor schools of thought. There are others. Jews are finding Jewish identity in small religious fellowships or *havurot*, in informal synagogues and home worship, and in a variety of religious, secular, cultural, social, and Zionist organizations. This American Jewish community is rich with choices and blessed with alternatives. Even within the four major religious movements there are many smaller schools of thought.

Surely each Jew can find a philosophy to satisfy a personal quest for Judaism and Jewish life. There is no reason for a Jew to turn aside to other religions for choice and option. All a Jew must do is to take advantage of the opportunities, study, live as a Jew, and choose. The greatest failing is not to choose but to fall away. It would be the final tragedy and most ironic failure if in this free land with its wide range of Jewish experiences, we were to somehow lose our interest in Judaism and the Jewish people.

The Torah has been compared to a tree of life for those who cling to it. No matter what choice you make, no matter which Jewish option you select, it can be *your* tree of life—if only you will cling to it.

GLOSSARY OF TERMS

Aliyah עֲלִיָה   An honor at the reading of the Torah in synagogue. Immigration to Israel.

Am Yisrael עַם יִשְׂרָאֵל   The Jewish people.

Bet Din בֵּית דִין   A Jewish religious court, usually consisting of three judges.

Brit בְּרִית   The Covenant; frequently refers to the covenant at Mount Sinai when Israel received the Torah.

Brit Milah בְּרִית מִילָה   Circumcision of males, normally on the eighth day after birth.

Eretz Yisrael אֶרֶץ יִשְׂרָאֵל   The land of Israel.

Galut גָלוּת   The scattered settlement of Jews throughout the world.

Gedolay hador גְדוֹלֵי-הַדוֹר   Great sages and yeshivah heads.

Get גֵט   A Jewish divorce.

Halachah הֲלָכָה   Jewish law.

Havurot חַבוּרוֹת   Small religious fellowships.

Hazzan חַזָן   The cantor who chants the synagogue prayers.

Heder חֶדֶר   A one-room Jewish school.

Kabbalah קַבָּלָה   Medieval Jewish mysticism.

Kaddish קַדִיש   Prayer of praise to God. Also, the mourner's prayer.

Kashrut כַּשְׁרוּת   Jewish dietary laws that assure that food is kosher (religiously proper).

Kehillah קְהִלָה   The organized Jewish community.

Keriah קְרִיעָה   Tearing of the garment as a sign of mourning.

Ketubah כְּתוּבָה   The Jewish marriage contract.

Klal Yisrael כְּלַל-יִשְׂרָאֵל   The world Jewish community.

Mahzor מַחֲזוֹר   The high holiday and festival prayer book.

Matmeed מַתְמִיד   A diligent student.

Mehitzah מְחִיצָה   A divider used in Orthodox shuls to separate men and women.

Melamed מְלַמֵּד Teacher.

Mezuzah מְזוּזָה A little box containing Torah passages placed on the doorpost.

Mikveh מִקְוֶה A ritual pool used for purification and conversion.

Minyan מִנְיָן A prayer quorum consisting of at least ten adult males.

Mitzvah מִצְוָה (plural: *mitzvot*) A religious commandment.

Mohel מוֹהֵל One who circumcises male infants according to Jewish ritual.

Semichah סְמִיכָה Ordination of a rabbi.

Shehitah שְׁחִיטָה Jewish ritual slaughter of animals.

Shivah שִׁבְעָה The seven-day mourning period for a near relative.

Shtiebel שׁטיבּל The Yiddish word for a one-room synagogue.

Shohet שׁוֹחֵט One who slaughters animals according to Jewish law.

Shul שׁול The Yiddish word for synagogue.

Shulhan Aruch שֻׁלְחָן עָרוּךְ The most important Jewish law code, edited in the sixteenth century.

Siddur סִדּוּר The prayer book.

Talit טַלִּית A prayer shawl.

Talmud Torah תַּלְמוּד תּוֹרָה An afternoon Hebrew school.

Tefillin תְּפִלִּין Two small leather boxes containing passages of the Bible. A male wraps tefillin around his head and arm for daily prayer.

Torah תּוֹרָה The Five Books of Moses: Genesis, Exodus, Leviticus, Numbers, and Deuteronomy.

Tzedakah צְדָקָה Charity.

Yarmulke יארמלקע A skull cap worn for prayer.

Yeshivah יְשִׁיבָה A Jewish all-day parochial school.

Yom Tov יוֹם טוֹב A Jewish festival.